D1219910

THE KEYS OF THE KINGDOM

A new strategy to change your life
and the world around you

PAUL M. GOULET

The Keys of the Kingdom

by Paul M. Goulet

Copyright 2013 – Paul Goulet

Published by RTM, Inc.

8100 Westcliff Dr.

Las Vegas, NV 89145

ICLV.com

Unless otherwise noted, all scripture quotations are taken from the New King James Version®. Copyright ©1982 by Thomas Nelson, Inc. Used by permission. All rights reserved.

Also unless otherwise noted, all Greek word translations and definitions are taken from *Biblesoft's New Exhaustive Strong's Numbers and Concordance with Expanded Greek-Hebrew Dictionary. Copyright (c) 1994, Biblesoft and International Bible Translators, Inc.*

The author has preferred to risk violation of certain grammatical rules, such as the capitalization of select proper names, rather than acknowledge the name of satan. Therefore, except in cases where the scripture was quoted exactly as printed in the Bible translation, satan and any related names are intentionally written in all lowercase letters.

Cover Design by Douglas Haines • Edited by Esse Johnson

All rights reserved under International Copyright Law. Contents and/or cover may not be reproduced in whole or in part or in any form without the express written consent of the publisher. If you would like to share this book with another person or persons, please purchase an additional copy for each recipient. Thanks for your respect and consideration.

ISBN: 0615952380
ISBN-13: 978-0-615-95238-3

CONTENTS

Preface

I'm thrilled to release *The Keys of the Kingdom* into your life, career, family and ministry. It's a message designed to take the principles of God's Kingdom beyond the walls of a local church and into the primary circles of influence and power in society.

In Luke chapter 10, Jesus told His followers, *"And heal the sick there, and say to them, 'The Kingdom of God has come near to you'" (Luke 10:9).*

The intention of our Savior was to transfer the Kingdom from heaven to earth through believers. Jesus taught His disciples only one prayer. In that prayer, He reaffirmed this intention:

> *Your Kingdom come. Your will be done, on earth as it is in heaven (Matthew 6:10).*

A few years ago, a man by the name of Lance Wallnau came to our church, ICLV (International Church of Las Vegas), to share his series of teachings. He calls it "The Seven Mountains Mandate." This mandate represents a new way of thinking about our purpose as believers. In it, Wallnau talks about "the seven mountains" of our world, which are the seven primary power centers, or spheres of influence, in our world system. Standing above them all is an eighth mountain, not of this world, which is intended to influence and dominate the others. This, of course, is the mountain of the Lord.

I really understood, applied and embraced Wallnau's teaching. Its message went hand-in-hand with my own conviction concerning the royal priesthood and the ministry of reconciliation.

But you are a chosen generation, a royal priesthood, a holy nation, His own special people, that you may proclaim the praises of Him who called you out of darkness into His marvelous light (1 Peter 2:9).

Therefore, if anyone is in Christ, he is a new creation; old things have passed away; behold, all things have become new. Now all things are of God, who has reconciled us to Himself through Jesus Christ, and has given us the ministry of reconciliation, that is, that God was in Christ reconciling the world to Himself, not imputing their trespasses to them, and has committed to us the word of reconciliation (2 Corinthians 5:17-19).

We've all been called to the ministry of reconciliation. For years, I've trained pastors and mentored other leaders in the ministry of helping hurting people. This is one of the secrets to ICLV's growth: lay counselors, whom we called *reconcilers*, were healed and empowered to bring health to their churches, homes and communities.

21 years ago, Denise and I moved to Las Vegas to lead a small, dysfunctional church, which just happened to be rented next door to a bar. I wasn't trained to be a lead pastor. I was a counselor. I loved counseling and training others to help the hurting multitudes, both inside and outside of the Body of Christ. The Seven Mountains Mandate aligned with my belief that ministry should happen every day, through every believer, in every situation. Christianity wasn't designed to remain within the four walls of a church. It was created to bring heaven to earth and people to heaven.

The mandate quickly became an important aspect of ICLV's DNA; but, as I taught it around the world, I realized I was uncomfortable with the limitation of seven mountains. I also felt that the analogy of *mountains* was restricting. Our world system looks more like kingdoms, and there are more than seven. In fact, there are many more and within each are spheres of control. Each carries a uniqueness that must be addressed.

If we're going to answer the call of Jesus to proclaim to the world that the Kingdom is near, we'd better know where it is and how to introduce people to it.

Within each one of us is a spiritual DNA lying dormant, just waiting for a set of keys to unlock our true potential and destiny. My dear friend, Eric Celerier, is the founder of the successful French website, TopChretien.Jesus.net. He recently told me that he'd "cracked the code" for a particular challenge.

I loved his analogy. Each problem in our families, churches, cities, businesses and nations, has a "code" that needs to be cracked. There are kingdoms that have been locked from the message of Christ. Eric has led over 6 million people to Christ in the past 6 years—he's cracked the code. Eric's got the keys to the internet kingdom. As a result, he's helped our church to explode into the online world. Thousands upon thousands are now watching our services and responding to the Word and the Spirit. It's so exciting! You can check out KnowingGod.net to see the English language version of this beautiful soul-winning tool.

We're all designed to release our spiritual DNA into our families and friends. The Apostle Paul knew that he had something to release that would unlock hearts, minds, cities and regions. That's why he wrote to the Romans, *"For I long to see you, that I may impart to you some spiritual gift, so that you may be established"* (Romans 1:11).

Paul was anxious to visit the Roman believers so that he could impart spiritual gifts into their lives. He knew he had power that could be transferred to them. He learned this, of course, from Barnabas, who probably learned it from Peter, who surely learned it from Jesus.

Your gifts, talents and anointing are given to you to unlock major spheres of influence in society. Many of these spheres have grown for hundreds of years. They're tarnished with generations of tradition, greed, lust, and even principalities and powers that are unseen.

For we do not wrestle against flesh and blood, but against principalities, against powers, against the rulers of the darkness of this age, against spiritual hosts of wickedness in the heavenly places (Ephesians 6:12).

God wants you to identify your unique set of gifts, talents and anointing so that you can influence the kingdoms that dominate this world. He wants you to possess the keys to unlock these kingdoms. Can you imagine what that will look like?

In the following pages, I believe that God's revolutionary principles will be revealed to you. Do you want to become part of His great strategy for this world? Do you know that He's calling you to overthrow the prince of the power of the air in order to establish His rule? The most amazing part of this is that He wants to do it through you.

Paul M. Goulet
Las Vegas, NV

INTRODUCTION
JESUS WANTS TO GIVE US
THE KEYS TO HIS KINGDOM

Jesus revealed that there were keys to a Kingdom called heaven when He prophesied into Peter's life:

> *Jesus answered and said to him, "Blessed are you, Simon Bar-Jonah, for flesh and blood has not revealed this to you, but My Father who is in heaven. And I also say to you that you are Peter, and on this rock I will build My church, and the gates of Hades shall not prevail against it. And I will give you the keys of the kingdom of heaven, and whatever you bind on earth will be bound in heaven, and whatever you loose on earth will be loosed in heaven" (Matthew 16:17-19).*

I wonder if Peter really understood the depth of these words. Did he grasp the implications and application of Kingdom keys? If I'd been in his sandals, I'm sure the concept would have flown over my head. In fact, for most of my Christian walk I was unable to grasp what Christ meant when He said, *"And I will give you the keys of the kingdom of heaven, and whatever you bind on earth will be bound in heaven, and whatever you loose on earth will be loosed in heaven" (Matthew 16:19)*. A few short years ago I began to comprehend: the promise is for me and every believer.

Thanks to Dr. Lance Wallnau and Bill Johnson, it dawned on me that Jesus has the keys of the Kingdom and He is willing to give them to every believer who wants to live a supernatural life. The keys were not just designed to build His Church; they were designed to bring the Kingdom of heaven to every life and every office, school, neighborhood, government and home. I believe this revelation will unleash a revolutionary move of the Spirit across every segment of our society. And, of course, into your personal life.

Do you remember the first day you picked up the keys to your new car, office or home? There was a rush of adrenaline and a sense of satisfaction as you crossed that threshold. Even though the bank or credit union may have loaned you the money to purchase the property, it still felt like it was all yours. By signing the loan documents, you assumed responsibility. You could use the property as you pleased, but only at a cost.

In Matthew 16:17-19, Jesus proclaimed to Peter that, one day, he would receive the keys of the Kingdom, and he would have the authority to bind and loose on earth just like He could in heaven. This promise was not just for Peter, but for every believer who confesses Christ as Savior and Lord. That confession opens a massive portal of blessings and authority.

When we make this type of heartfelt declaration, Jesus starts the process of turning over the Kingdom of heaven to us, His heirs. Perhaps some of you have received keys to a car or home as a gift or inheritance. Those keys were real. They opened real doors to real property. The keys of the Kingdom are just as real. Their purpose is to unwrap the incredible gift that the Father wants to give to you because of His love.

> *For God so loved the world that He gave His only begotten Son, that whoever believes in Him should not perish but have everlasting life (John 3:16).*

Jesus Christ is the rightful heir to the Kingdom of heaven because He is the only begotten Son of the Father. This incredible privilege is then shared with us because Christ calls us His friends:

> *You are My friends if you do whatever I command you (John 15:14).*

He holds us tight in His hands and calls us joint heirs:

> *...and if children, then heirs—heirs of God and joint heirs with Christ, if indeed we suffer with Him, that we may also be glorified together (Romans 8:17).*

He promised to give us the keys of the Kingdom:

> *And I will give you the keys of the kingdom of heaven (Matthew 16:19).*

The Keys Of The Kingdom Are For...

The keys of the Kingdom unlock wealth, health, joy, peace and love, which permanently dwell in heaven. They open the door that releases the atmosphere of heaven into a life and world so dark and polluted. Have you ever opened the door to your house to let fresh air in or stale air out? Have you ever opened a door in your house to allow light to enter a room? Of course. We all have.

Christ gives us keys that enable us to open the heavens in order to release angelic forces, creative powers and healing. Malachi 3:10, for example, teaches us that tithing opens the windows of blessings from heaven:

"Bring all the tithes into the storehouse, that there may be food in My house, and try Me now in this," says the LORD of hosts, "If I will not open for you the windows of heaven and pour out for you such blessing that there will not be room enough to receive it" (Malachi 3:10).

God promised to pour out a blessing we can't contain. Sounds awesome to me! We see in Malachi this principle of unleashing heaven's resources on earth.

If tithing can unleash heavenly finances, what can love, faith, mercy and obedience release? Remember that it is the Father's will to give you the keys,

Do not fear, little flock, for it is your Father's good pleasure to give you the kingdom (Luke 12:32).

And that we should pray daily for His will to be done on earth,

Your Kingdom come. Your will be done, on earth as it is in heaven (Matthew 6:10).

What are you waiting for? Let's go deeper into this revelation.

It's Time To Invade The Earth

Jesus wants to give you and me the keys of the Kingdom because He wants us to establish His Kingdom on earth like it is in heaven. Although, today, there are fewer *literal* kingdoms on this earth with real kings and queens, this message is even greater in the 21st century. I love the words of the song "Something About That Name" by Gloria and William J. Gaither, which proclaim this message so well: *"Kings and kingdoms will all pass away, but there's something about that name."*[1]

There are kingdoms that cross geographical boundaries to influence every society, regardless of language or ancient tradition. I'm referring to the kingdoms of finance, education, family, religion, science, medicine, sports, music, television, the internet, arts, entertainment and government.

We can actually keep adding to the list. I've taught the *seven mountains* concept for years without being convinced that I could squeeze every power source into only seven big categories. After taking a closer look at the Word and the realities of a world that doesn't fit such a small box, I've expanded the list. I also speak of *kingdoms* rather than mountains.

I'm aware that the initial thought of the seven mountains came in a dream from a well-respected Christian leader. Please don't get me wrong— I'm not criticizing those who've taught the seven mountains. I'm immensely grateful for the revelations they've introduced. The Seven Mountains Mandate was a great place to start, but it needed to be expanded. Doesn't the Word say, *"The kingdoms of this world have become the kingdoms of our Lord and of His Christ, and He shall reign forever and ever"* (Revelation 11:15b)?

In other words, identifying the very real kingdoms of our world is essential to cracking their code. How will you influence the kingdom of film if you don't recognize that very specific traditions, practices and laws govern it? What about professional soccer or football? These sports represent multi-billion dollar industries that have huge societal and economic significance around the world. They have not only geopolitical, but also spiritual elements that need to be addressed. They're very real kingdoms.

Who's targeting them? What set of gifts, talents and anointing are required to make a difference in those arenas?

Crack The Code

Who's going to crack the code of film? dance? education? medical research? Each kingdom needs to be targeted. Intercessory prayer needs to be unleashed in order to address the powers and principalities entrenched behind the scenes. The gifts of the Spirit need to be expressed. Words of knowledge and wisdom are critical for effective strategy meetings. The gift of the discerning of spirits is vital when creating strategic partnerships, and identifying spiritual and political alliances. We all need the gift of faith while implementing vision.

I could easily spend the next few chapters identifying each gift and talent required to implement a well thought-out, spiritual approach to cracking the code for every kingdom that we could think of, but then I'd be doing your work. It's your calling to take these principles and apply them to your kingdom context.

I was recently sitting at a coffee shop studying the Word and listening to worship music. (Every morning, I love to sneak away for two or three hours of prayer, Word and meditation.) As I studied in 1 Timothy, I discovered that Paul grasped this principle 2,000 years ago:

This charge I commit to you, son Timothy, according to the prophecies previously made concerning you, that by them you may wage the good warfare, having faith and a good conscience, which some having rejected, concerning the faith have suffered shipwreck (1 Timothy 1:18-19).

Paul encouraged his spiritual son, Timothy, to war the "kalos" war, also translated the *good* or *beautiful* war.

The Greek term for war, "strateuo," is actually used three times in this verse. It's the root of our English word *strategy*. In this case, he was telling Timothy to use the prophetic words from his past to do warfare. *Beautiful warfare!*

It's important that we spend more time strategizing. Then we'll have a more significant impact on every strata of society. I don't believe that, as Christians, we're called to hide from the world. We're supposed to influence it and bring the Kingdom into every field, classroom, science lab, business, arena and political power center.

My wife, Denise, and I are privileged to have three amazing kids. We love them so much. In 2004, we also opened our home and hearts to two teenagers from Africa. Joseph is 6 feet 8 inches and Fernand is 7 feet tall. We have a full home; full of love and vision. As parents, it's our desire and prayer that our kids will learn how to have a significant impact on the kingdom they're called to. Each of them has their own special mix of gifts, talents and anointing. It's been our mission to help them discover their DNA to influence the kingdoms of their world. Whether in the realm of high school basketball, college, worship, film, counseling or business, each one has a specific mission field in life. I can assure you that each of these realms is resistant to change. The power structures that control them are stubborn. Some are spiritual, and some are carnal. Paul warned us that our battle is not against flesh and blood (Ephesians 6:12). You'll have to fight to influence a kingdom that doesn't want to be taken over by a bunch of Christians. Jesus even said,

And from the days of John the Baptist until now the kingdom of heaven suffers violence, and the violent take it by force (Matthew 11:12).

I'm not advocating violence, of course; however, Christians must develop a more global and strategic approach to world transformation. If Jesus really prayed "Your Kingdom come," then perhaps we need to partner with His desire and prayer? What do you think? Have we really made it our life's mission to crack the code of every kingdom of this world, so that we can implement His Kingdom on earth? Please forgive me if I seem facetious. Now that I've got this concept clearly in my mind and spirit, it irritates me that for so long Christians have been content to argue about "stuff," or wallow in offense rather than change the world.

Maybe I'm being radical, but Jesus did promise that *"... on this rock I will build My church, and the gates of Hades shall not prevail against it" (Matthew 16:18).* Let's park our churches on the gates of every kingdom—even the gates of hell. Let's train our children to be the next crop of scientists, educators, inventors, doctors, humanitarians, athletes and world leaders.

A few years ago, I was driving my grandson Luke home from preschool at ICA (International Christian Academy). I was surprised and pleased when he asked this amazing question, "Papa, what should I do with my life?"

I laughed for a moment because I've asked him this question since he was just a toddler. I always talk about vision and destiny with my kids and grandkids.

This was the first time he'd asked for my opinion. My answer came quickly, "Luke, Papa can't tell you what to do with your life. Ask the Lord, and I'll do my best to help you accomplish it."

As we drove a few more minutes in silence, Luke seemed satisfied with my answer. Then, he shouted out the words I'll never forget, "Okay Papa, I know what I want to do with my life..."

I was so excited that I shouted with great joy, "What is it?" Five years old and he already knew his life mission. Wow! Praise God.

"Luke, what is it?"

He answered with crystal clear assurance, "Papa, I want to be Spider-Man."

I laughed so hard I needed a moment to regain my composure. Then I said, "That's cool, Luke. Can Papa be Batman?"

You should have seen the look on his face!

"No Papa, you're too old."

Wow! What a bummer!

It's not strange for my family to talk about callings and destiny at five years old. It's part of our tradition. It's become part of our church's DNA. I'm hoping and praying that it will become part of your DNA.

The Kingdoms Are Up For Grabs

Control of these kingdoms is up for grabs. For years, Christians saw their role in a myopic fashion. Our vision was so limited. Our methods were so dated. Our confidence was weak. *The Keys of the Kingdom* is written to inspire and release you into God's great mission for you. Your true purpose and significant eternal impact will not necessarily be accomplished behind a pulpit or a piano. The Holy Spirit is tired of being confined to church buildings. He wants to hit the streets through you. He wants to work through you to influence and change the kingdoms.

There's no longer a divide between sacred and secular. Everything is new. Everything can be invaded by the sacred.

I'm so grateful to the individuals who've been living this reality. They've inspired me to want more for my family, church and city. My contact with John Maxwell, Dr. Augustine Pinto, Dr. James Marocco, Dr. Bill Bright, Dr. Richard Dobbins, Dr. David Lim, Chuck Pierce, Lou Engle, and so many more have taught me that the power of the Spirit of Jesus will create a Kingdom atmosphere anywhere. In fact, the life of Jesus demonstrated that wherever He went, so did the Kingdom of heaven. If the message of this book can help you bring the Kingdom of heaven to every classroom, theatre, conference room, studio, kitchen and law office, then it will have achieved its ultimate goal. Enjoy, apply and love this great message.

Questions:

1) Do you believe that God has placed you in the position that you're in, or that you're in your present situation through someone else's disobedience?
2) Do you believe that God wants to use you right where you are to establish His Kingdom?
3) Are you ready to receive the keys of the Kingdom?

ENDNOTES

1. Copyright 1970 William J. Gaither, Inc. (Admin. by Gaither Copyright Management). Quoted with special permission.

1
WHAT IS GOD'S WILL FOR YOUR LIFE?

Have you ever wondered if God has a perfect will for your life? If you could discover this will, would you do your best to fulfill it no matter the cost? Would you be willing to surrender yours to embrace His? What if God showed you His will for your family, city, state, or nation - would you join His plan in big and small ways?

I hope that all these questions have intrigued your mind. If you've never asked yourself these questions, then you've probably never sought to hear His will for yourself or others. In my estimation that would be very sad. Every child of God has been redeemed for a purpose. Every man or woman that has been used by God first established a desire to seek and to do God's will.

Even though King David made big mistakes, his personal dedication to knowing and obeying the will of God for his life was clear,

> *Give me understanding, and I shall keep Your law; indeed, I shall observe it with my whole heart. Make me walk in the path of Your commandments, for I delight in it (Psalm 119:34-35).*

David was the only man that God called a man after His own heart,

I have found David the son of Jesse, a man after My heart, who will do all My will (Acts 13:22b, also see 1 Samuel 13:14),

and the apple of His eye,

Keep me as the apple of Your eye (Psalm 17:8a).

What a great example for us to follow.

Jesus Christ also expressed this same motivation in the only prayer that He taught his disciples, *"Your will be done on earth as it is in heaven"* (Matt 6:10). We've all prayed and recited this prayer countless times and, yet, how many of us truly know what we're praying...*and mean it?*

Notice that Jesus wanted to daily seek the will of God, *Your Kingdom come. Your will be done.* Without a doubt, Jesus made it a priority to seek God's will for this world and to establish it *on earth as it is in heaven.*

In other words, when we seek, pray for and obey God's will, we help to establish His Kingdom here on earth. Since His will is already being done in heaven, Jesus wants believers to establish God's will on earth.

Is this your deepest longing? When I was first saved, my biggest concern was to do the will of God. This desire consumed my thoughts and feelings. I read articles and books on how to find it. I wanted it for me and my family, but I didn't understand how to bring the Kingdom of God to a broken world. Although I tried to get everyone saved, I was happy just to get ready for the rapture. Back then, we weren't getting saved to change our world. We were getting saved to avoid the tribulation and hell. Now that it's been over 30 years, I've realized that I was saved from hell to bring the Kingdom of heaven to wounded people, cities and nations.

I'm sure that in the Garden of Gethsemane when Jesus prayed, *"Father, if it is Your will, take this cup away from Me,"* He was demonstrating that same principle. He could've been spared the pain and humiliation. He had the authority to call a legion of angels to save Him and wipe out the hypocrites and soldiers. Instead, He saw the big picture as He spoke these famous words:

...nevertheless not My will, but Yours, be done (Luke 22:42b).

Our wills are often focused on comfort, self-preservation, pride or ambition. His will directs us to the good of others. In Christ's case, His will would have let the cup of pain, rejection and humiliation pass. However, He made a declaration of His choice to do the will of the heavenly Father instead of His own. Isn't that the same decision we all have to make at different times in our lives? Isn't that what Lordship is all about?

Choosing His will instead of our own is the main point of accepting Christ as Savior *and* Lord. As Savior, He saves us from our sin; but as Lord, He calls the shots for our purpose and destiny. In other words, He saves us *from* something *for* something. He saves us *from* sin *for* a world move of His Spirit, which He has planned to do through us.

Our daily concern, motivation and prayer should be, "Hey Dad, I want Your will for my life, family, business, school, church and government, and today I need Your Holy Spirit to fill me in order to help me establish Your Kingdom here. I'm not sure how this is going to happen, but I know that You will teach me, lead me and empower me."

2
THE KINGDOM EXPANSION IN YOU

The purpose of this book is to help you tap into some of the revelations that God has shown my wife and me over the past few years. He is truly leading us in His ways and by His Spirit. The churches, orphanages, schools, ministries and people that have been built or transformed through the International Church of Las Vegas are a testament to His involvement in our lives.

I often feel like Apostle Paul, *"For I know that in me (that is, in my flesh) nothing good dwells,"* with the exception, of course, of the Spirit of Jesus Christ. (Romans 7:18) I'm amazed at what God has done in and through us. At the age of 20, I wanted to die. Caught in a world of anger, depression, alcohol and drugs, I searched for the true meaning of life.

When I couldn't find it in friends, family, success, achievements, pleasure and all that the world had to offer, I became despondent. Once the party was over, I was still empty. Drugs, alcohol, entertainment, possessions and pleasures are only opiates designed to numb the pain of a Christ-less soul.

All of these memories are easily accessible to me. I don't have to look far to remember how I felt then, and how desperate I am now, without the favor of God and the presence of the Holy Spirit. Remember that He saved us *from* something *for* something. Without His daily presence and our surrender to His will, we can easily slip back into a shallow life. Do I have to mention the names of men and women who were once greatly used by God, but somehow their lives became a shambles due to pride, presumption, ego, lust or greed?

In his first epistle, John warned of three forces that can trip any one of us if we stray from His Lordship:

> *For all that is in the world—the lust of the flesh, the lust of the eyes, and the pride of life—is not of the Father but is of the world (1 John 2:16).*

Those three forces can shipwreck anyone that doesn't surrender to the daily leading of His presence. God, help us to scream out the prayer that You taught us more than 2,000 years ago:

> *And do not lead us into temptation, but deliver us from the evil one (Matthew 6:13).*

Take a moment and speak this entire prayer in your own words, expressing its incredible intent. This is what my prayer sounds like:

Hey, Dad, I love you so much. You're my real Father in heaven. Every time I think of You I feel humbled and amazed that You love me. Even the mention of Your name still gets to me. Father, wow. What a privilege it is to me to be in relationship with You.

Hey, Dad - I don't like the way this world is going. Please have Your will in my life and this world. Please use me to establish Your Kingdom power, principles and laws in strategic places that You have sent me to. I really want Your Kingdom to infiltrate every kingdom of this world.

Hey, Dad, You know that I have physical, emotional, financial and spiritual needs. Please supply all my needs with superabundance so I can be generous on all occasions.

Hey, Dad, forgive me for all the stupid things I've done, said and thought. Forgive me for the times I failed to do the good that I could do. Forgive me for ever grieving the Holy Spirit. Cleanse me and show me Your grace and mercy over my life, family and church.

Hey, Dad, I choose today to forgive all those that have offended, hurt, cheated, lied to, or angered me in any way. I also forgive all those who have hurt the ones I love. I hand them over to You. Please don't hold it against them. You've been so gracious to me.

Hey, Dad, You know that I still struggle with temptations. I don't really trust myself that much, but I do trust You. Would You do me a big favor? Would You lead me away from that stuff? In 1 Corinthians 10:13, You promised me a way of escape. Wow, thanks. I really need that assurance.

Hey, Dad, while I'm representing You today on this earth, and while I'm being used by You to establish Your Kingdom, please deliver me from the counter attacks of the evil one. He really has it in for my family and me. Please protect my wife, kids and grandkids. I know that I can count on You.

Hey, Dad, by the way, You are awesome and incredible. You deserve all the praise and glory of every kingdom and every soul. There is no way to measure Your worth or give You enough praise. I guess that all I can do is give You all of me, all of my kingdoms. Take me today and use me for Your glory and praise. Amen.

Application:
Take a moment to write out your prayer.

Friends, we don't have to use fancy words to talk to our Father. Jesus wasn't concerned with perfect prayers, but with a clean heart in relationship with the Father. He welcomed us into that intimate relationship. Wow. Can you feel this truth?

The other ingredient that we so desperately need is the power to accomplish His will. Yes, first we need to *want* His will. Then we need to *discover* His will. And then we need to *accomplish* His will. Bringing God's will to the earth in the same measure that it's being done in heaven isn't easy. We'll have to displace principalities and powers in high places. We can't accomplish this with just a good plan or lots of personal charisma. It has to come by the Holy Spirit and His power through us.

In my book, *The 5 Powers of God*, I biblically establish that God has five distinct powers which He wants to deposit into your life to help you accomplish the mission that He's given you. In Mark 16:15, Jesus gave us our marching orders when He said, *"Go into all the world and preach the gospel to every creature."* Most Christians call this the great commission. Notice the word that is used, "co-mission." Hence, we have a mission that can only be successful if we do it with Him; i.e., *co*-mission.

Although the great commission is for every believer, God has unique assignments for each of us. The commission is fulfilled when we fulfill our individual and corporate assignments. The five powers of God are available to us in order to accomplish our assignments for His glory.

These are the five powers of God to accomplish our mission:

Dunamis is the miracle working power of Jesus. It's available for miracles, breakthroughs and healings.

Exousia is the power of authority. It's useful for us to overcome fear and intimidation and is required for spiritual warfare and expansion.

Energeia is God-energy that flows through us to accomplish various tasks. It's also present during times of worship or prayer when people say they "feel" His presence.

Kratos is God's dominion power. Ultimately, He wants to reign and rule over all of His creation. We need kratos power to bring the Kingdom of God down to the earth. Whenever His Kingdom expands on Earth, we're looking at His kratos power dominating the scene.

Ischus is the strength sent from God for times when we are weak or tired, or when temptation knocks on our door. Ischus helps us to resist.

The Keys of the Kingdom builds upon this revelation of the five powers of God. I hope and pray that, through these pages, you'll be thoroughly equipped to fulfill the will of God in your life, ministry, business and family.

Are you ready to embark on a new journey? Don't forget that revelation always leads to transformation.

Questions:
1) Do you know God's will for your life?
2) What do you enjoy doing?
3) What gifts and talents do you have that God could use?
4) Have you ever experienced the power of God?

3
WHAT IS THE FATHER'S PLAN FOR US?

In Luke 12, Jesus revealed that it is the Father's pleasure to give us the Kingdom:

Do not fear, little flock, for it is your Father's good pleasure to give you the kingdom (Luke 12:32).

Wow! This Scripture tells me God's plan for my life, family and church. When I first received Christ, I was told by staff members from Campus Crusade for Christ that God had a wonderful plan for my life. I never could've imagined that His plan included giving me His Kingdom.

Jesus knew that this was always the intent of the Father. When He taught His disciples how to pray, I'm sure they were shocked by the key themes He identified. Let's look at the prayer once again to discover these revolutionary themes.

So He said to them, "When you pray, say:

Our Father in heaven, hallowed be Your name. Your kingdom come, Your will be done on earth as it is in heaven. Give us day by day our daily bread and forgive us our sins, for we also forgive everyone who is indebted to us. And do not lead us into temptation, but deliver us from the evil one" (Luke 11:2-4).

Theme 1: Our Father...

Not my, but *our* Father. Jesus was including us as children of God. He was also calling Him our *Father*. The direction of the prayer was a child talking to a father. Wow. That must have blown the minds of the religious people who were afraid to even say Lord or Jehovah. To call God *Father* must have sounded disrespectful or sacrilegious.

Theme 2: Our Father in heaven...

Jesus was making it clear that our true Father lives in heaven. We all have earthly fathers who've fulfilled their role either well or poorly. Some of us were even scared by them, but Jesus leveled the playing field when He said, *"our Father."*

Theme 3: Hallowed be Your name...

To "hallow" something is to regard it as holy and set apart. Praising the Father and honoring His name as utterly holy is not only appropriate, it's necessary. He deserves all of our praise.

Themes 4 & 5: Your kingdom come. Your will be done on earth as it is in heaven...

Jesus wasn't advocating a cool prayer life, whispered by weak believers, who are hiding in the corners of their little church. He was letting everyone know His agenda right up front. He was saying, "Father, establish Your Kingdom here on earth and overthrow the earthly kingdoms."

These disciples were training to pray earth-changing prayers. Jesus was raising an insurgency against the kingdoms of this world. He wasn't revolting against Roman rule; He was revolting against the devil's rule over this planet. Didn't Paul call him "the prince of the power of the air"?

And you He made alive, who were dead in trespasses and sins, in which you once walked according to the course of this world, according to the prince of the power of the air, the spirit who now works in the sons of disobedience (Ephesians 2:2).

The daily prayer of every believer should be revolutionary. We should pray, "God, I'm not in love with the kingdoms of this world. Use me, my family and my church to establish Your Kingdom. I don't want my will or my ways of doing stuff. I want Your will in every area of who I am!"

This type of thinking requires a real paradigm shift. We're no longer pew-sitting believers, clinging to the superstars, trying to be perfect in an imperfect world. We're now armed-and-dangerous spies on a mission from God to help establish heaven on earth by the power of the Holy Spirit.

The keys of the Kingdom will always center us on this paradigm that is so foreign to the thinking of most Christians. That's why this mind transformation is prerequisite. Not only is it His pleasure to give us His Kingdom, but God has a plan and strategy to empower you to accomplish your mission.

See, I have set before you an open door, and no one can shut it (Revelation 3:8).

The keys revealed in this book will help open doors that no man can shut. They'll help you conquer personal, social, national, financial, moral and emotional problems. Quit praying survival prayers and start praying revolutionary prayers.

Questions:
1) Do you see God as your Father?
2) Are His plans for your good? If so, why?
3) Are you bringing the Kingdom of God down to this earth? If so, how?
4) Take a moment to write the most revolutionary prayer you can, in your own words, expressing your strongest faith declarations:
> -What would you like to see changed in your world and sphere of influence?
> -Do you know that this is the Father's plan? If so, how do you know?

4
THE FOUR TYPES OF GOOD NEWS

Have you ever thought about your purpose in God's great plan for the universe? Do you fit in? Did He plan you before He created the heavens and the earth? What about the purpose of the Church? Why should we go to church? What should we be doing? Is your purpose clear? Is the Church's purpose clear?

The Good News About Salvation

The term "gospel" means *good news*. *Salvation* comes from the Greek word, "sozo,"[1] which means *to save, deliver, or protect*.

When I was eighteen years old, I heard the gospel of salvation for the first time. No one had ever told me about the born-again experience, or my need to receive Jesus Christ into my life.

> *But as many as received Him, to them He gave the right to become children of God, to those who believe in His name: who were born, not of blood, nor of the will of the flesh, nor of the will of man, but of God (John 1:12-13).*

As a child, I truly believed in God, but I never gave Christ free access into my mind and spirit. A personal relationship with Christ was totally foreign to me. One night, a group called "Athletes in Action" gained permission to share this good news with our college hockey team after evening practice. I'm not sure why the coach allowed it, but I'm glad he did. Two weeks later, I received Jesus as my personal Savior. This started a brand new journey into the good news of salvation. I got saved from depression, saved from my empty lifestyle, saved from myself and saved from an uncertain future.

I quickly plugged into Campus Crusade for Christ. I learned to memorize the "Four Spiritual Laws"[2] and "The Romans Road."[3] Immediately, the leaders taught me how to share my new faith in Christ. For the next two years, I immersed myself in the good news of salvation. It was awesome. Jesus had given me personal peace and freedom. I was saved now, and everyone else needed this message.

My amazing transformation from a hard hockey player to a gospel preacher wasn't an easy journey. I found strength in the Word and incredible Christian friends who helped me along the way. I'm forever grateful.

Shortly before the passing of Campus Crusade's founder, Bill Bright, I had the privilege of kneeling at his bedside and thanking him for his role in my life. If it hadn't been for the staff members at Campus Crusade, I probably would never have heard the gospel of salvation. As I continued my journey in Christ, I had a million questions. I questioned my Catholic theology, the evangelical beliefs that were being taught to me, and my psychology classes at the University of Ottawa. My world had been shaken, but I knew that Jesus was real.

Questions:
1) Have you ever invited Jesus Christ into your life and body to become your Savior and Lord?
2) If so, when did you invite Him in? If not, be assured:

As many as I love, I rebuke and chasten. Therefore be zealous and repent. Behold, I stand at the door and knock. If anyone hears My voice and opens the door, I will come in to him and dine with him, and he with Me (Revelation 3:19,20).

Go ahead. Ask Him to forgive and fill you.

The Good News About The Holy Spirit

Eventually, I stumbled upon verses in the Bible about the Holy Spirit. What was the baptism of the Holy Spirit? What about the day of Pentecost? What about miracles and healings in the Bible? Nobody that I knew was talking about this kind of stuff. We were too busy trying to win people to Jesus, but Acts 1:8 piqued my interest. So, I started asking others about it. Although no one ever deterred me from my journey, none of my friends had ever experienced the baptism of the Holy Spirit.

But you shall receive power when the Holy Spirit has come upon you; and you shall be witnesses to Me in Jerusalem, and in all Judea and Samaria, and to the end of the earth (Acts 1:8).

I had this little blue "Holy Spirit" book by Bill Bright, and it gave me the direction I needed. After a few months of fervent seeking, I was filled with the Holy Spirit! It was so great. The next few years of my life concentrated on the good news about Jesus and the need for a second experience in the Spirit.

As my personal pilgrimage with Christ continued, it became clear to me that there *had* to be more than the messages of salvation and the baptism of the Holy Spirit. I'd met too many people who received Christ and the Holy Spirit, but were still crippled emotionally and relationally. This realization led to the next chapter of my journey: *the message of reconciliation.*

Question:
Have you been baptized in the Holy Spirit?

"Baptism" means *completely immersed*. If you ask Him, He will totally fill you and immerse you in His Spirit.

If you then, being evil, know how to give good gifts to your children, how much more will your heavenly Father give the Holy Spirit to those who ask Him! (Luke 11:13)

The Good News About Reconciliation And Inner Healing
Reconciliation comes from the Greek word "katallage,"[4] which means *exchange, restoration, divine favor.*

Therefore, if anyone is in Christ, he is a new creation; old things have passed away; behold, all things have become new. Now all things are of God, who has reconciled us to Himself through Jesus Christ, and has given us the ministry of reconciliation, that is, that God was in Christ reconciling the world to Himself, not imputing their trespasses to them, and has committed to us the word of reconciliation. Now then, we are ambassadors for Christ, as though God were pleading through us: we implore you on Christ's behalf, be reconciled to God. For He made Him who knew no sin to be sin for us, that we might become the righteousness of God in Him (2 Corinthians 5:17-21).

I realized that a born-again Christian who'd been baptized in the Holy Spirit still needed personal, spiritual and relational healing. I then spent the next ten years helping people get healed, reconciled and whole. This message of Christ as *healer* became the theme of my life and ministry. I can tell you that we were able to help many people through our Sunday school, college classes, counseling sessions and *The Breakthrough Series*, which was a series of classes that I wrote to facilitate healing and emotional health in believers. The series has evolved into two important training tools.

The first of the two was the *Healthy Leaders* series, which helps leaders become healthy spiritually, emotionally and relationally. It then gives them the tools to help others.

The second series was designed to help people heal using three 30 day intensives entitled *The Thirty Day Journey to Spiritual Health*, *...to Emotional Health*; and, finally, *...to Relational Health*. The workbook and video series facilitates the healing power of the Holy Spirit to flow through people's lives. The results have been incredible.

In 1992, God called my wife and me to pastor a small church in Las Vegas. As a first time senior pastor, I only knew three messages:

1. You must receive Jesus Christ
2. You should be baptized in the Holy Spirit
3. You can encounter Jesus as the healer of your family, marriage and life.

That was the extent of my life journey—three themes that I believed were true. For the first year-and-a-half in Las Vegas, I concentrated on these messages. They were the core values of my life. I was familiar with them and confident in their truth.

Jesus Talks About His House

In like manner, Jesus spent the first 15 chapters of Matthew talking about the subject that was near and dear to Him—the gospel (good news) of the Kingdom (His home before his birth). Don't forget that, in the beginning, Jesus was with the Father. When Genesis 1:26 says, *"Let Us make man in Our image, according to Our likeness...,"* we see the amazing relationship between the Father and the Son. Furthermore, Jesus' role in creation was revealed in Colossians:

For by Him all things were created that are in heaven and that are on earth, visible and invisible, whether thrones or dominions or principalities or powers. All things were created through Him and for Him (Colossians 1:16).

The gospel of John again highlighted the Father-Son role in creation,

In the beginning was the Word, and the Word was with God, and the Word was God. He was in the beginning with God. All things were made through Him, and without Him nothing was made that was made (John 1:1-3).

We can, therefore, fully conclude that Jesus knew everything about the Kingdom of heaven. His mission on earth was to reveal His true identity, equip and empower future leaders, die for our sins, rise again, and interlock heaven and earth.

This is where you and I come into the picture. In the first 15 chapters of Matthew, Jesus imparted to His disciples a clear understanding of what heaven is like. The principles of heaven formed Jesus' core values. Once this clear foundation was set, Jesus gave His disciples a pop quiz, *"Who do men say that I, the Son of Man, am?"* (Matthew 16:13)

Peter, of course, got an A+ on this quiz when He said, *"You are the Christ, the Son of the living God."* (Matthew 16:16) His declaration opened the door to more revelation.

Questions:
1) Have you allowed the Holy Spirit to bring you into seasons of reconciliation to God, self and others?
2) Have you been healed of all your hurt and anger?
3) Has Christ firmly established the Kingdom of heaven in you?

ENDNOTES

1. Sozo, NT: Strong's #4982
Please note: Every Greek or Hebrew word study in this book, unless otherwise specified, is taken from Biblesoft's New Exhaustive Strong's Numbers and Concordance with Expanded Greek-Hebrew Dictionary. Copyright (c) 1994, Biblesoft and International Bible Translators, Inc. Greek terms will be referenced with the Greek word followed by the Strong's Concordance Number.

2. "Four Spiritual Laws" is a Christian tract, which is a pamphlet typically used as a tool for evangelism. This tract is designed to teach the essentials of the Christian faith through four succinct "laws." You can view the tract on Campus Crusade's website here.

3. "The Romans Road" is also a tract. It was and remains a popular way to present the gospel of salvation using only scriptures from the book of Romans.

4. Katallage, NT: Strong's #2643

5
THE GOOD NEWS ABOUT
THE KINGDOM OF GOD

From that time Jesus began to show to His disciples that He must go to Jerusalem, and suffer many things from the elders and chief priests and scribes, and be killed, and be raised the third day (Matthew 16:21).

Notice that it says, "from that time on." From *what* time? From the time when Jesus had given Peter and the disciples the keys to His Kingdom. In other words, Jesus spent 15 chapters of Matthew teaching them how to drive the car and, in Chapter 16, He finally handed over the keys. Then, from Matthew 16 to Matthew 28, Jesus built upon the Kingdom foundation that He laid down in the first 15 chapters.

Isn't this exciting? Jesus transitioned the message because the disciples were ready to graduate. They finally understood the A, B, C's of changing the world:

A) Let Me tell you about My Kingdom.

B) Let Me tell you what I am about to do.

C) Let Me show you what I have to do.

D) Let Me give you what you need to change the world.

It seems so amazing to me that the Kingdom message isn't clearly taught in most churches. If Jesus started with these truths, why don't we practice them? Let's take a moment to talk about why He started His teaching ministry with the Kingdom message.

The Five Reasons Jesus Taught About The Kingdom Of God

1. Jesus was very familiar with the Kingdom of heaven. It was and is His true home.

   In the beginning was the Word, and the Word was with God, and the Word was God. He was in the beginning with God (John 1:1-2).

2. He entered a religious system that had almost completely distorted the truth. As the representative of the Kingdom, Jesus wanted to set the record straight.

   Woe to you, blind guides, who say, "Whoever swears by the temple, it is nothing; but whoever swears by the gold of the temple, he is obliged to perform it." Fools and blind! For which is greater, the gold or the temple that sanctifies the gold? And, "Whoever swears by the altar, it is nothing; but whoever swears by the gift that is on it, he is obliged to perform it." Fools and blind! For which is greater, the gift or the altar that sanctifies the gift? Therefore he who swears by the altar, swears by it and by all things on it. He who swears by the temple, swears by it and by Him who dwells in it. And he who swears by heaven, swears by the throne of God and by Him who sits on it (Matthew 23:16-22).

3. He needed to change the end times theology of the Jews. All of the Jews expected the coming Kingdom and the coming King. They'd been waiting for hundreds of years. Many were sincerely wrong about who and how their king would be; they had misinformed expectations. They weren't expecting a suffering Messiah. Jesus had to clean up their theological end times mess.

4. A clear understanding of the keys of the Kingdom would help His followers implement Kingdom realities here on earth. This was Jesus' intention from the beginning.

   Your Kingdom come. Your will be done on earth as it is in heaven (Matthew 6:10).

5. Teaching them the keys of heaven would help the believers to see God as their Father, instead of as a cruel tyrant.

In this manner, therefore, pray: Our Father in heaven, hallowed be Your name (Matthew 6:9).

Jesus was concerned about our relationship with God:

If you had known Me, you would have known My Father also; and from now on you know Him and have seen Him (John 14:7).

The concept of God being a Father to a believer was revolutionary to the Jews. In Matthew 16, Peter made a realization and confession that would forever change his life.

He said to them, "But who do you say that I am?"

Simon Peter answered and said, "You are the Christ, the Son of the living God" (Matthew 16:15-16).

New Revelation

My wife and I just celebrated our 20th anniversary as pastors of our church, and 33 years of marriage. We're getting old, aren't we? When my parents celebrated their 25th anniversary, I thought they were so old. I guess I was wrong, wasn't I? Ouch!

It seems that, in the past year, the lights have been going on for me. I'm getting revelation that is rocking my boat and enhancing the way I lead ICLV.

My recent epiphany began while listening to teachers like Bill Johnson and Dr. Lance Wallnau, who've been talking about the Kingdom of God invading the earth. Wow, the Kingdom *invading* earth. Sounds radical, doesn't it? Ignited, I embarked on a journey of study and prayer that would eventually yield a clear understanding of the gospel of the Kingdom, and our goal to download heaven to earth. Let's walk through the highlights of this revelation.

The Big Transition: Revelation Leads To More Revelation

From that time Jesus began to show to His disciples that He must go to Jerusalem and suffer many things from the elders and chief priests and scribes, and be killed, and be raised the third day (Matthew 16:21).

Something caused Jesus to introduce a new aspect of His life message in Matthew 16. It was "from that time" that Jesus began talking about His upcoming suffering and resurrection. This was a clear break from His previous teachings. It's not that He abandoned the first series of teachings; He was simply building upon a clear understanding of the Kingdom. In other words, His disciples couldn't learn about the gospel of salvation until they fully grasped the gospel of the Kingdom of heaven.

You see, none of us was allowed to go to college until we graduated from high school. You couldn't take calculus until you grasped algebra. Matthew 16:21 marked a day of graduation, a day of transition, where the disciples finally recognized who Jesus was. He was the promised Messiah and the coming King. Peter's confession helped to unlock another level of revelation.

Exercise:
List 10 descriptive terms that would summarize Jesus' teachings about the Kingdom of heaven.

Questions:
1) How did Jesus *live* these 10 principles in His earthly ministry?
2) How have you lived these principles in your own life?

6
THE BIG REALIZATION:
THE DAY THE LIGHTS WENT ON

He said to them, "But who do you say that I am?"

Simon Peter answered and said, "You are the Christ, the Son of the living God" (Matthew 16:15-16).

Peter's confession of Jesus as the Christ proved to Christ that the lights were finally going on for at least one of His disciples. Historically, they all believed in the gospel of the Kingdom. Like all good Jews, they were waiting for a messiah that would be their king, free them from Roman rule and re-establish the throne of David. Their beliefs about the coming messiah were embedded in their identity, their theology, their lifestyle. They couldn't view Jesus any other way. Our suffering Messiah came in such sharp contrast to their belief structure that it took 15 chapters to change their minds about the real Kingdom of heaven.

Only after correcting their understanding of God's Kingdom could Jesus reveal a side of Himself that they'd never seen—the Messiah who had to suffer and die for their sins. Trust me; this was not a popular message among a people waiting to be saved from their earthly turmoil.

Peter's confession affirmed that Jesus was truly breaking through hundreds of years of misconception and deception. The Lord's response to this confession revealed His ultimate plan. I call it "The Big Plan."

Jesus Reveals "The Big Plan"

Look at this incredible sequence of events. Peter confessed Jesus as the Christ and the living God. Jesus then blessed him and declared the source of Peter's insight:

Jesus answered and said to him, "Blessed are you, Simon Bar-Jonah, for flesh and blood has not revealed this to you, but My Father who is in heaven" (Matthew 16:17).

Jesus knew it came from His Father and He blessed Peter for tapping into the revelation stream. He then spoke into Peter's life and highlighted the significance of his confession. Based on what Peter proclaimed, Jesus prophesied:

And I also say to you that you are Peter, and on this rock I will build My church, and the gates of Hades shall not prevail against it (Matthew 16:18).

Somehow, Simon Peter had tapped into revelation from God the Father. I believe that God has more revelation like this for you.

Once again, revelation confessed always unlocks further revelation. Further revelation always releases greater authority. Jesus gave Peter the keys of the Kingdom of heaven so that he could unleash Kingdom power and principles *on earth as in heaven.*

This reminds me of the day I handed the keys to a Mustang convertible to my daughter, Christine, on her 16th birthday. It was a thrill, and she deserved it. She was, and still is, a real woman of God. Although she had the keys, I still owned the car—and the car payments. As long as she obeyed my wife and me, she was given the privilege to drive it.

It also reminds me of the story in Luke 10 when the seventy returned with a good report:

Then the seventy returned with joy, saying, "Lord, even the demons are subject to us in Your name." And He said to them, "I saw satan fall like lightning from heaven" (Luke 10:17-18).

Jesus saw the impact of their actions in the spirit realm. The Greek word translated as *saw* is "theoreo,"[1] which means *to be a spectator of, discern, experience, or intensively acknowledge.*

It means that Jesus was a spectator of the dynamic impact of their ministry. It's kind of like a parent who sits on the sidelines of their child's soccer match. I guarantee you they feel every emotion of every game. God feels the same way when we walk in faith and power. Praise God for a heavenly Daddy that is proud of us.

God wants to see us excel. He wants us to succeed. He cheers when we have victories and picks us up when we fail. The Holy Spirit is called the "Paraclete." He's the One called to come alongside us, offering help and comfort when we need it.

Jesus Gave Them Keys To Accomplish The Plan

Jesus responded to the success of the seventy's mission by giving them a clear promotion.

> *Behold, I give you the authority to trample on serpents and scorpions, and over all the power of the enemy, and nothing shall by any means hurt you (Luke 10:19).*

This was consistent with the parable in Luke when the master says, *"Well done, good servant; because you were faithful in a very little, have authority over ten cities" (Luke 19:17).*

Wow, isn't that amazing? Jesus often gives us more after we've been faithful with a little. That's what the original text means. You were faithful with *puny* stuff; behold, I'll make you responsible for lots of stuff. Remember that God gives us more authority when we're faithful in the tasks He delegates to us. Never despise the day of small things (Zechariah 4:10). Revelation in small matters leads to great authority.

ENDNOTES

1. *Theoreo*, NT: Strong's #2334

7

WHAT IS THE KINGDOM OF GOD?

In order for the disciples to understand the level of Christ's authority and the need for His death, they had to have a clear picture of His heavenly Kingdom. The gospel of salvation is completely based on the truths and realities of heaven. This is why, in the first 15 chapters of Matthew, Jesus labored to set such a clear foundation.

And Jesus went about all Galilee, teaching in their synagogues, preaching the gospel of the kingdom, and healing all kinds of sickness and all kinds of disease among the people (Matthew 4:23).

After overcoming satan in the wilderness, Jesus clearly defined His message. It was the truth about heaven. In other words, He started talking about His Daddy's Kingdom.

Have you ever left home for an extended period of time? I have. On every trip, the longer I'm gone, the more I miss home, and the more I talk about my family, my friends, my neighbors, the smells, the food and my church. It's normal to want to talk about home. It was normal for Jesus, too. At first, all He wanted to do was to tell about His home: heaven.

While I was a teenager, my dad received an offer to move to Belgium to lead a large, struggling corporation. Even though it was in the middle of the school year, I had no choice; Europe would be our new home. I'll never forget how much I missed my friends, the food and the lifestyle. Searching for American products and food became a minor obsession. Finding like-minded people also became a huge issue. Even the smell of American peanut butter tremendously alleviated my longing for home.

Jesus must have felt the same way. Home was heaven, perfect in every way. Israel was a mess. The world was a mess. Don't you think He wanted a lot more of heaven on this crazy globe?

The only way that He could make the earth more like His real home was through believers who understood where He was from, and where He wanted to take them. Jesus taught His disciples to pray for the Kingdom of heaven to take over the world order. The primary goal of our existence is to bring heaven to earth and snatch souls away from the devil.

Let's dissect Jesus' prayer one more time to illustrate that His home was the foundation of everything He did.

In this manner, therefore, pray: Our Father in heaven, hallowed be Your name. Your Kingdom come. Your will be done on earth as it is in heaven. Give us this day our daily bread. And forgive us our debts, as we forgive our debtors. And do not lead us into temptation, but deliver us from the evil one. For Yours is the kingdom and the power and the glory forever. Amen (Matthew 6:9-13).

1. The prayer was directed to *Our Father.*

It makes sense doesn't it? His closest relationship was with the Father. The eternal connection had been the Father, the Son and the Holy Spirit. Jesus didn't say, "*My* Father who is in heaven." He started with "*Our* Father." If God *the* Father is *our* Father then it opens up so many important revelations. The fact that God is my Father means that I can have an intimate relationship with Him. If He's my Daddy, I must also have His DNA in my body. Aren't we created in the image of God? Wow, this is incredible! Jesus wasn't being exclusive. He was letting us into the most important relationship of all time. We can ask our Daddy anything in Jesus' name:

In that day you will ask in My name, and I do not say to you that I shall pray the Father for you; for the Father Himself loves you, because you have loved Me, and have believed that I came forth from God. I came forth from the Father and have come into the world. Again, I leave the world and go to the Father (John 16:26-28).

2. He asked His Daddy to establish His Kingdom on earth like it is in heaven.

Now remember that heaven is BIG. It's so big that astronomers estimate it contains over 100 billion galaxies and is still expanding. This is not 100 billion planets, but 100 billion galaxies. In other words, Jesus is saying, "Hey, Dad, You're so great. You reign over all the galaxies. How about doing something with this rebellious little planet where satan is temporarily in charge? Let's rock this earth through these disciples."

Are you getting this yet?

3. The Father's will is already being done in the heavens.

Jesus underlined the fact that His Daddy's will is always being done in the 100 billion galaxies and, therefore, should also be done here. But God's will is not being done on earth right now. There are millions of babies aborted, millions of children being abused, and millions are dying from disease and war. People have often asked, "Why does God allow this?" The answer is so simple: God gives us free will. With this power to choose we can bring life or death, good or evil. We can either love or hate this world of ours. It comes down to a choice. Don't forget that satan also has a free will; he's still actively trying to steal, kill and destroy.

> *The thief does not come except to steal, and to kill, and to destroy. I have come that they may have life, and that they may have it more abundantly (John 10:10).*

The first request in the prayer of Jesus dealt with asking His Daddy and our Daddy to bring His will, His truths, His power to this earth, just like in heaven. The prayer that Jesus taught His disciples portrayed the ultimate purpose of our existence—to bring the Kingdom of heaven to this earth.

Jesus did come to destroy the works of the devil. He did come to raise up an army of believers that are called to join Him in this final battle.

> *For this purpose the Son of God was manifested, that He might destroy the works of the devil (1 John 3:8b).*

The Radical Message Was Not Well-Received

Jesus' message was challenged by the religious hypocrites. They couldn't fathom a world that included everyone in God's love and acceptance. Their world was full of prejudice, legalism and self-righteousness. Jesus threatened their perspective on the Kingdom by demonstrating His incredible grace.

> *Then one was brought to Him who was demon-possessed, blind and mute; and He healed him, so that the blind and mute man both spoke and saw. And all the multitudes were amazed and said, "Could this be the Son of David?"*

> *Now when the Pharisees heard it they said, "This fellow does not cast out demons except by Beelzebub, the ruler of the demons."*

But Jesus knew their thoughts, and said to them: "Every kingdom divided against itself is brought to desolation, and every city or house divided against itself will not stand. And if I cast out demons by Beelzebub, by whom do your sons cast them out? Therefore they shall be your judges. But if I cast out demons by the Spirit of God, surely the Kingdom of God has come upon you" (Matthew 12:22-28).

Everywhere Jesus went, He preached about the establishment of God's Kingdom on earth. The zealots loved this message because they thought He would be enthroned by military force. The everyday Jew loved it because it gave them hope in the midst of their life of Roman oppression and religious darkness.

The Message About The Heavenly Kingdom Shook The Earthly Kingdoms

We know that His message was being distorted by the religious leaders, but that didn't stop Jesus from sharing it wherever He went. Not only did Christ share about the power of His Daddy's Kingdom, He demonstrated it with healings and miracles. Everyone but the religious hypocrites loved the demonstrations. The multitudes followed Him because He taught with authority and He had compassion on them. Jesus' compassion caused Him to love people and confront legalists:

Blind guides, who strain out a gnat and swallow a camel (Matthew 23:24).

Jesus Confronted Religious Strongholds

Direct confrontation with the religious rulers of His time did not make Christ popular with the establishment. He didn't have an earthly plan to gain the approval of people. Instead, He exercised divine authority over sickness, death and the doctrines of men.

When the Kingdom of heaven invades this earth, it comes into direct opposition with the kingdoms of this world. Paul the Apostle understood this dynamic when he said, *"For we do not wrestle against flesh and blood, but against principalities, against powers, against the rulers of the darkness of this age, against spiritual hosts of wickedness in the heavenly places" (Ephesians 6:12).*

When Jesus, the King of kings, entered a region of demonic oppression, people and demons reacted. Jesus demonstrated that His Kingdom was greater through miracles, healings and deliverances. It's not a mystery that Jesus could bring heaven's resources to earth because, as He said,

All authority has been given to Me in heaven and on earth (Matthew 28:18).

Our Lord is called the King of kings (Revelation 17:14). Every other king and kingdom must submit to him.

And as he was still coming, the demon threw him down and convulsed him. Then Jesus rebuked the unclean spirit, healed the child, and gave him back to his father (Luke 9:42).

The demons knew who Jesus was, and they knew that their time was soon approaching. Jesus' Kingdom was greater. He proved it by the authority that His Kingdom had, which ruled over demonic powers.

And suddenly they cried out, saying, "What have we to do with You, Jesus, You Son of God? Have You come here to torment us before the time?" (Matthew 8:29).

They knew that their time of final judgment was coming one day. They also knew that Jesus had the ability to torment them.
Wow! Isn't that powerful?

Jesus Delegated Authority

Behold, I give you the authority (exousia) to trample on serpents and scorpions, and over all the power (dunamis) of the enemy, and nothing shall by any means hurt you (Luke 10:19-20).

Not only did Jesus have authority, but He could also hand this authority to His followers. Our delegated authority in Christ is far greater than the devil's power. Yes, the devil has power, but we have greater authority.

Jesus demonstrated this and then delegated it to His followers. He couldn't give what He didn't have. He had *all* authority, so He was able to give it away to people like you and me. Jesus even had the power to forgive. No one had ever claimed this type of authority to forgive sins.

When Jesus saw their faith, He said to the paralytic, "Son, your sins are forgiven you." And some of the scribes were sitting there and reasoning in their hearts, "Why does this Man speak blasphemies like this? Who can forgive sins but God alone?" (Mark 2:5-7).

Jesus claimed to be from a Kingdom where the rulers, laws and principles took precedence over the rulers of this earth. He was bringing a set of Kingdom laws that had more authority than natural laws. Jesus said, *"Do not think that I came to destroy the Law or the Prophets. I did not come to destroy but to fulfill" (Matthew 5:17).*

Jesus' teaching and actions illustrated not only the apparent nature of the Kingdom, but also that it could invade this present world. He didn't like their nice little religious world. His methods drove the religious experts crazy. Why didn't He fit in? Why did people hate the Christ so much? Why did their religious people want to kill Him? The answer is clear—Jesus wasn't from this place. He came from another kingdom.

Do you understand how important this is? You and I have been adopted into a family that is from another place. Its values are very different from the ones where we live now. We're not called to be assimilated into this world. We're called to establish an extension of our new Kingdom into the worldly kingdoms.

My dad was a hero in World War II. As a paratrooper in the 1st Special Forces, he and many other troops invaded the beaches of Anzio to dethrone the kingdom of Mussolini and Hitler. Their mission was clear. It was violent because satanic kingdoms do not give up easily. The allied forces didn't come to be assimilated. They came to liberate people and establish democracy.

Here's another illustration. As I mentioned earlier, Denise and I recently became legal guardians of two foreign exchange students. Joseph and Ferdinand came from Rwanda, a nation that has experienced one of the greatest genocides in recent history.

Our kids were moving out. Our eldest had married; our second daughter was moving into her own home; while our youngest, Samuel, had only two years of high school left. We weren't sure that we were done pouring into kids yet. Should we adopt a child? Should we have another child? We didn't know exactly what God was trying to tell us. All we knew was that we were blessed and had more to give.

Through a series of events, the opportunity to house one foreign exchange student was presented to us, and we jumped at it. It was an incredible blessing for us and this young man. Eventually, we invited another Rwandan to join our happy family. I can assure you, there've been some adjustments for Joseph, Ferdinand and the whole family. I've gotten used to people staring at us. I'm white; they're black; and they're both about one foot taller than me. And while we've all had to adjust, I can also assure you that our two Rwandans did not come to establish Africa here in Las Vegas. They've had to adapt to our culture. They're not on a mission to establish their kingdom in the US. They've come to glean from all the blessings of living in the US.

For a while, my wife prepared breakfast for them and our son Samuel every morning. Four or five eggs each, pancakes and whatever else we could find. We needed to rearrange our grocery runs and refrigerator to accommodate our new friends.

They've had to adjust to the English language, the American lifestyle and so many other mysteries. Although they love their homeland and families, their mission wasn't to bring their kingdom and culture here to America. It was to get a great education and maybe become great basketball players. But as Christians, the purpose of our mission is very different. We do come from a great place. And we do have much authority.

Do not love the world or the things in the world. If anyone loves the world, the love of the Father is not in him (1 John 2:15).

Jesus Was Super Human

Recently at our church, while teaching about the gospel of the Kingdom, I tried to find an illustration that everyone could grasp, and that would demonstrate that Jesus came from another place. Its laws are different; its atmosphere is different; its economy is different; even its source of light is different. Come to think of it, His Kingdom is in another time zone, *"But, beloved, do not forget this one thing, that with the Lord one day is as a thousand years, and a thousand years as one day" (2 Peter 3:8).*

These facts made me think about Superman. As a child, he was just a normal kid being raised on a planet called Krypton. His parents sent him to earth moments before their planet was destroyed. When he landed on earth, he was rescued and raised by a kind family. Little did they know that eventually their little alien boy would become a super human. On Krypton, he would've had a normal existence, but on earth, his DNA caused him to have enough power to defy natural laws and make the world a better place.

Jesus wasn't really from this planet, and Joseph wasn't really His daddy. Jesus wasn't really only 33 years old when He was killed. He was eternally existent.

In the beginning was the Word, and the Word was with God, and the Word was God. He was in the beginning with God. All things were made through Him, and without Him nothing was made that was made (John 1:1-3).

Jesus Had A Heavenly DNA

Jesus was there when the earth was created. He was there when Isaiah saw the Lord. Jesus can be found throughout the Old Testament. Theologians call these phenomena "Christophanies." Jesus, the man, demonstrated that He was made more than a man. He had super human abilities.

He could walk on water:

Now in the fourth watch of the night Jesus went to them, walking on the sea (Matthew 14:25).

He could turn water into wine:

And He said to them, "Draw some out now, and take it to the master of the feast." And they took it. When the master of the feast had tasted the water that was made wine, and did not know where it came from (but the servants who had drawn the water knew), the master of the feast called the bridegroom. And he said to him, "Every man at the beginning sets out the good wine, and when the guests have well drunk, then the inferior. You have kept the good wine until now!" (John 2:8-10)

He could multiply a few fish and loaves of bread into a feast for thousands:

He said, "Bring them here to Me." Then He commanded the multitudes to sit down on the grass. And He took the five loaves and the two fish, and looking up to heaven, He blessed and broke and gave the loaves to the disciples; and the disciples gave to the multitudes. So they all ate and were filled, and they took up twelve baskets full of the fragments that remained. Now those who had eaten were about five thousand men, besides women and children (Matthew 14:18-21).

He could quiet a storm and calm the sea:

Then He arose and rebuked the wind, and said to the sea, "Peace, be still!" And the wind ceased and there was a great calm (Mark 4:39).

Like Superman, the fact that He was from another place enabled Him to supersede the laws of nature that limit us. Earth's laws couldn't control Jesus; He was destined to rule and reign as King of kings and Lord of lords.

Are You A Citizen Of The Kingdom Of God?
You see, the Kingdom of heaven is greater than the kingdoms of this world. The principles and the power of the Kingdom of heaven are greater than the worlds'. Every one of us has to decide which master we'll submit to. You have to declare your citizenship—you can't serve two masters.

No servant can serve two masters; for either he will hate the one and love the other, or else he will be loyal to the one and despise the other. You cannot serve God and mammon (Luke 16:13).

You have to decide who your daddy is going to be. Whom will you bow down to? Who will be your king? Once you choose God, you'll automatically come under His jurisdiction—His laws and His authority. Bob Dylan wrote a powerful song, "You've Got to Serve Somebody,"
"You've got to serve somebody. Well you can serve the devil or you can serve the Lord but you got to serve somebody."[1]
Whom will you serve? Isn't that the greatest question of all time? The core of all human problems?

Millennia ago, satan entered the Garden of Eden. He managed to con two unsuspecting humans into compromise and disobedience. Eventually, this serpent convinced humans that his reasoning was greater than God's:

Then the serpent said to the woman, "You will not surely die. For God knows that in the day you eat of it your eyes will be opened, and you will be like God, knowing good and evil" (Genesis 3:4-5).

Satan became the ruler of this world through cunning lies and manipulation. Jesus came to change all of this, and the Father gave Him all authority to get mankind back on the right track:

And Jesus came and spoke to them, saying, "All authority has been given to Me in heaven and on earth" (Matthew 28:18).

You Have Been Given Great Authority

Behold, I give you the authority to trample on serpents and scorpions, and over all the power of the enemy, and nothing shall by any means hurt you (Luke 10:19).

Authority defined: "exousia"[2]— privilege, force, capacity, competency, freedom, or mastery (concretely, magistrate, super human, potentate, token of control), delegated influence.

Power defined: "dunamis"[3]—force, specially, miraculous power.

Go therefore and make disciples of all the nations, baptizing them in the name of the Father and of the Son and of the Holy Spirit, teaching them to observe all things that I have commanded you; and lo, I am with you always, even to the end of the age. Amen (Matthew 28:19-20).

Because Jesus had all authority and delegated it to His followers, we were called to go. The authority is there for us to take back territory that satan has stolen.

As born-again, Spirit-filled believers, we're destined to take back our rightful place as primary influencers and transformers of this society.

We can bring Kingdom laws and powers to a world whose ruler has left it in chaos. Satan is the Saddam Hussein over the government of this world. Our mission is to dethrone the liar who has deceived the entire world. The Father, Son and Holy Spirit are still asking from heaven, *"Whom shall I send, and who will go for us?"* (Isaiah 6:8)

Exercise: List 5 attitudes of Jesus that prove that He was from another world.

Question: As a citizen of heaven, what rights do you have on this earth while you are here.

ENDNOTES

1. Copyright 1979 by Special Rider Music. Quoted with special permission.

2. *Exousia*, NT: Strong's #1849

3. *Dunamis*, NT: Strong's #1411

8
ARE YOU AN ALIEN FROM ANOTHER PLANET?

For our citizenship is in heaven, from which we also eagerly wait for the Savior, the Lord Jesus Christ, who will transform our lowly body that it may be conformed to His glorious body, according to the working by which He is able even to subdue all things to Himself (Philippians 3:20-21).

Are we aliens from another planet? The answer to this question is, of course, no. However, we are aliens from another kingdom.

If Christ is from another kingdom, what happens to us when He takes residence in our bodies, minds and spirits? When you invited Jesus Christ into your heart, did you believe that He came into your body? What did He do once He entered your body? He transformed you from a regular person into a child of God.

But as many as received Him, to them He gave the right to become children of God, to those who believe in His name: who were born, not of blood, nor of the will of the flesh, nor of the will of man, but of God (John 1:12-13).

Not everyone is a child of God, as some suggest. Jesus told the religious rulers that their daddy was the devil (John 8:44).

Believe defined: "pisteuo"[1]—to have faith in, upon, or with respect to, a person or thing, by implication, to entrust (especially one's spiritual well-being to Christ).

When you believed in Christ and received Him into your life, where do you think He went? Into your body, of course. When you invited Christ to come into your life, He did so by sending His Spirit to live inside of you:

> *Do you not know that you are the temple of God and that the Spirit of God dwells in you? (1 Corinthians 3:16).*

Do you realize that the day you asked Jesus into your life He actually entered into your body? You have the Holy Spirit of Jesus living inside of you. In both thought and deed, He's transforming you to look like Jesus.

Question:
Have you ever invited the Holy Spirit of Jesus into your life and body?

> *Behold, I stand at the door and knock. If anyone hears My voice and opens the door, I will come in to him and dine with him, and he with Me (Revelation 3:20).*

Jesus is banging on the door of your life. He wants to fill you with His Spirit. Without Him, you have no power to obey or even love Him. But once He fills you with His Spirit, a metamorphosis begins. You're instantly born of the Spirit—enabled to love and do the will of God.

> *That which is born of the flesh is flesh, and that which is born of the Spirit is spirit (John 3:6).*

Once you're born again, or "born of the Spirit," you have become spiritually alive. You're no longer the same person.

In Ephesians 2:5, Paul explained it this way,

> *...even when we were dead in trespasses, [God] made us alive together with Christ (by grace you have been saved).*

Then later in Ephesians 2:13,

> *But now in Christ Jesus you who once were far off have been brought near by the blood of Christ.*

And further in Ephesians 2:19,

Now, therefore, you are no longer strangers and foreigners, but fellow citizens with the saints and members of the household of God.

When you received the Spirit of Jesus into your body, you became an alien in this world. Now you're just passing through. Your ultimate residence is in heaven. In fact, there's a dimension in you that can already draw from your heavenly resources to live an abundant life here on earth.

Blessed be the God and Father of our Lord Jesus Christ, who has blessed us with every spiritual blessing in the heavenly places in Christ (Ephesians 1:3).

As an alien in the earth, you have rights in heaven. Once you've invited the Spirit of Jesus to live in your body, your personal identity and purpose in life changes.

For you did not receive the spirit of bondage again to fear, but you received the Spirit of adoption by whom we cry out, "Abba, Father." The Spirit Himself bears witness with our spirit that we are children of God, and if children, then heirs—heirs of God and joint heirs with Christ, if indeed we suffer with Him, that we may also be glorified together (Romans 8:15-17).

And since we have the same spirit of faith, according to what is written, "I believed and therefore I spoke," we also believe and therefore speak, knowing that He who raised up the Lord Jesus will also raise us up with Jesus, and will present us with you (2 Corinthians 4:13-14).

Your relationship with God as your Father is established when the Spirit of Jesus fills you. Then, your spiritual DNA begins to change you from the inside out. Because you now have His Spirit, your thoughts and behavior will begin to reflect His character. Don't forget that the Holy Spirit is the Spirit of Jesus. He will only take control of your life as you surrender to Him. Evil spirits, on the other hand, will gladly control a person.

But the Holy Spirit will only fill us and lead us if we surrender to His process. This Spirit-led process will help you become the world changer that God designed you to become. Once you receive His spiritual DNA, you're pre-designed to grow in the Lord, and to change your life and the lives of those around you.

Are you willing to make this choice today? If you haven't yet, invite Him to fill you, forgive you and change you forever.

You've Been Promoted To Ambassador: You Represent The Kingdom Of God Wherever You Go

Now then, we are ambassadors for Christ, as though God were pleading through us: we implore you on Christ's behalf, be reconciled to God (2 Corinthians 5:20).

Ambassador defined: "presbeuo"[2]—to be a senior, act as a representative.

When you allow the Holy Spirit to take control of your life, you begin to walk in a new authority and earthly position. This earthly position is that of an ambassador for our King. An ambassador is a representative of the ruling authority. As people who've been forgiven of sins, filled with the Spirit of Jesus, and changed by His power, we're called to represent in this world the interest of our homeland and our King.

Our daily prayer to our Father in heaven is *"Your will be done, on earth as it is in heaven" (Matthew 6:10)*. When we pray this way, we align ourselves with God's will. He wants us to represent Him here on earth. We've been assigned the title of ambassadors with all the rights, powers and privileges that go along with it.

What are the rights, powers and privileges of our position? Good question. I'm glad you asked. Get ready for a serious identity lift. You've heard of a facelift, haven't you? Well this reality is an identity lift. You can never see yourself the same way after you embrace this truth.

The Rights, Powers And Privileges Of An Ambassador

And I will give you the keys of the kingdom of heaven, and whatever you bind on earth will be bound in heaven, and whatever you loose on earth will be loosed in heaven (Matthew 16:19).

Bind defined: "deo"[3]— to bind (in various applications, literally or figuratively).

Loose defined: "luo"[4]— to loosen (literally or figuratively).

Jesus clearly promised Peter the keys of the Kingdom of heaven. Keys always symbolize authority or the ability to unlock something. What are the keys that Jesus was alluding to? How could these keys help us bind and loose here on earth? Could it be that the keys are the secret that will help us bring the Kingdom of heaven down to the earth? Is this really the will of God for His ambassadors: to bring heaven's laws, powers and reality to their earth? Is this what Jesus did and taught while He was on the earth? *Aren't these great questions?* In the next chapter, we'll get some answers to each one of these questions before we describe the keys in detail.

ENDNOTES

1. *Pisteuo*, NT: Strong's #4100

2. *Presbeuo*, NT: Strong's #4243

3. *Deo*, NT: Strong's #1210

4. *Luo*, NT: Strong's #3089

9

THE KEYS TO ESTABLISH AND EXPAND THE KINGDOM ON EARTH

Have you ever wondered what these keys look like? Are they made of gold encrusted with diamonds and rubies? Are they translucent? Or are they invisible principles that can be used by any disciples of Jesus Christ? Let's look at some of these keys.

Key #1: A message
The disciples were given a message to preach.

And as you go, preach, saying, "The kingdom of heaven is at hand" (Matthew 10:7).

They were initially only given one message. Wow, it must have been important, and it still is. They didn't need a PhD to spread the message. It was simple. It probably sounded something like this:
"Hey buddy, I've got to tell you something."
The unsuspecting Jew would have been curious, "Sure. What is it, brother?"
"My Master told me to tell you that the Kingdom of heaven is near."

I'm sure he would have asked, "Who's your master?"

The disciple of Jesus would then pronounce with confidence: "Jesus."

Everyone in Israel knew about Jesus. The signs, wonders and miracles were too big to hide. These were all signs of the Kingdom. It surely built their level of expectation. If the Kingdom was near, then blessings, miracles and healings were, too.

Don't forget that this is your first key: the Kingdom within you is greater than the kingdom of this world. You and I can share and demonstrate this great message today.

Key #2: Power

Power is the demonstration of God's Kingdom power over the kingdoms of this world. Jews understood that there were heavenly powers and demonic ones. Our message would be mere words if we couldn't back it up with power. Jesus did.

Key #3: Authority

Then He called His twelve disciples together and gave them power and authority over all demons, and to cure diseases. He sent them to preach the Kingdom of God and to heal the sick (Luke 9:1-2).

Remember:

Power defined: "dunamis"— force, specially, miraculous power.

Authority defined: "exousia"— privilege, force, capacity, competency, freedom, or mastery (concretely, magistrate, super human, potentate, token of control), delegated influence.

-He gave them power and authority over all demons.
-He gave them power and authority to cure diseases.
-They were sent to preach the Kingdom of God and heal.

The disciples weren't preaching salvation yet. They didn't understand or even know of it, and they were still unsure of Jesus' true identity. They preached what Jesus had taught them; namely, the Kingdom of God.

With the preaching came the demonstrations of Kingdom power by exercising Christ's authority. If you're going to proclaim that your kingdom is bigger and better, you'd better prove it. That's exactly what the disciples did. When I was in grade school, I used to brag that I was tough. I had to prove it many times, too many times. I learned to keep my big mouth shut if I wasn't willing to back it up.

I also had the recourse of saying that my dad was tougher than theirs. Because he was from the Special Forces, I knew I wasn't exaggerating. It seems ironic that I still brag about my heavenly Father.

As Christians, we don't have to keep our mouths shut. We've got the keys of the Kingdom, and we can tell everybody about it. And not only tell them, but we can prove it. Jesus *told* us to prove it.

Most assuredly, I say to you, he who believes in Me, the works that I do he will do also; and greater works than these he will do, because I go to My Father (John 14:12).

Key #4: A mission

Heal the sick, cleanse the lepers, raise the dead, cast out demons. Freely you have received, freely give (Matthew 10:8).

Jesus gave us the power and authority freely so that we would give it away freely. Our mission is to give it all away.

Even Paul the Apostle, a second generation follower, a post-resurrection believer, a post-ascension believer, understood that the message was central, but the power was the proof:

And my speech and my preaching were not with persuasive words of human wisdom, but in demonstration of the Spirit and of power, that your faith should not be in the wisdom of men but in the power of God (1 Corinthians 2:4-5).

Paul taught the message of salvation and the message of the Kingdom, and He demonstrated both. Do you understand both messages? Can you back up your beliefs with power?

For the Kingdom of God is not in word but in power (1 Corinthians 4:20).

The message of salvation saved their soul and changed their destiny. The message of the Kingdom gave them a purpose to live and die for.

Key #5: The Spirit-filled life

For as many as are led by the Spirit of God, these are sons of God (Romans 8:14).

If we live in the Spirit, let us also walk in the Spirit (Galatians 5:25).

The Spirit-filled, Spirit-led life is completely amazing. When He leads us, we have access to the gifts and the fruit of the Spirit. Our lives are different.

Paul never stopped getting closer to the Spirit of Jesus. This was his primary focus because he knew it was the only way to fulfill his mission:

...that I may know Him and the power of His resurrection, and the fellowship of His sufferings, being conformed to His death, if, by any means, I may attain to the resurrection from the dead (Philippians 3:10-11).

Questions:
1) Is this like your life? Have you received the good news of salvation but neglected the good news of the Kingdom?
2) Is it God's will for the followers of Jesus to bring the Kingdom of heaven to earth?
3) Have you accessed the powers of God for your life and ministry?
4) Are you intimate with the Holy Spirit?

10
HISTORICAL TRENDS:
IS THIS A NEW MESSAGE
OR A NEW REVELATION?

I've been alive long enough to see the body of Christ go through some significant changes. The world has experienced massive changes. As a whole, the Body of Christ has shifted its emphasis, methods and message many times through the centuries. As a whole, the Catholic Church has had a fairly aggressive role in establishing Kingdom principles in society. Although there have been countless abuses and aberrations of justice that do not reflect the Spirit of Jesus Christ, we've also seen mainline denominations help to establish the foundations of most democratic nations and legal systems.

We see the birth of art, education, science and medicine fostered by religious fervor and resources. Some of our greatest schools and hospitals have been started by people of noble spiritual character. These people had a grasp of bringing Kingdom principles to their earth. When Moses received the Ten Commandments, he was instituting Kingdom laws on this earth. Every great revival since the reformation has had a dramatic effect upon society, government, laws, education, the arts, the family and the Church.

The Message Of The 70s And 80s

In the early 1900s, the message of the born-again experience concentrated primarily on the Pentecostal baptism of the Holy Spirit. Catholics and Protestants were both impacted by this good news.

Then, in the 70s and early 80s, the Church's message concentrated on the end times. And in recent history, the birth of the evangelical movement shifted the Church's message to personal salvation. The born-again experience became about personal decisions for Christ and subsequent personal transformation. It seemed that the good news of salvation was being preached without the gospel of the Kingdom.

This message failed us. I heard it said about those years, "We are not polishing brass on a sinking ship." It was a time when Christians retreated to the safety of their communities and the four walls of their churches. Our only relevance to the leaders of industry and government was spiritual. Our only goal was to get them saved. Evangelicals would scream out, "Don't miss the rapture! Don't go to hell!" The Pentecostals would say, "Get baptized in the Holy Spirit, speak in tongues, or *feel* the power of God."

While we were getting saved and baptized in the Holy Spirit, while we argued about the end times or the gifts of the Spirit, the Church became almost irrelevant. During that time, I never heard a message that encouraged us to enter politics, start businesses and build wealth; or to develop media expertise, influence the arts, or study law or the sciences.

It seems to me that the overall attitude was to abandon the sinking ship. Unfortunately, we almost completely retreated into our own little worlds. Although I'm only looking back about 30 years, I realize that, unknowingly, we were giving up on the world. *The beast was coming. Armageddon was around the corner.* We weren't trying to establish Kingdom principles, power and presence in our courts, schools, government and nations. Instead, we retreated into our comfortable denominations or fellowships to congratulate ourselves on the great work we were doing.

We must have been winning some of the world to Jesus because our churches experienced growth and our budgets increased. We built buildings and filled the pews. But we weren't changing society.

I lived through the 60s, 70s, 80s, 90s and even the great day of Y2K. There were only a few pioneers that tried to be relevant in society. My mentor, Dr. James Dobson, integrated psychology with our faith. He dared to *focus on the family.*

I remember the leaders that encouraged me to forsake my dream of getting my master's degree in psychology. *Jesus was coming any day.*

Would we, the Church, be further ahead if we'd filled the courts, schools, businesses, government, hospitals, counseling centers and homes with the people who were filled with Jesus' Spirit, love, wisdom and power? Wouldn't the world have become a better place?

What would've happened if we'd measured our success by the change in society rather than the size of our churches?

The 80s And 90s Shift

In the late 80s and 90s, there seemed to be a radical shift in some evangelicals. People like Pat Robertson and Jerry Fallwell got involved in the political arena. People of faith started expressing political and legal opinions that represented the Spirit of Christ rather than the spirit of the world (or even the anti-Christ spirit).

People like Dr. Dobson, Dr. Dobbins and Gary Collins applied the message of Christ to the family. This kingdom of the family had been overtaken by the psychological theories of Freud, Rogers and Jung. It was time for the Church's message to shift.

Today, it's common for Christians to influence every kingdom of this world. "Politics" is no longer a dirty word in churches. Christians are challenging the legal systems. They're becoming salt in the judicial process. Could it be that the Church is leaving the dark ages of irrelevancy?

This may stir a few of you! I believe that the Word of Faith movement which has been ridiculed by many evangelists has, in fact, had a major impact on the realm of business and finances. Their emphasis on personal prosperity challenged the Church to think differently. Suddenly, these preachers were telling believers that God wanted them to be successful. He wanted them to be financially blessed. In other words, while you're storing up treasures in heaven, you can also enjoy a life of prosperity and blessings. Paul the Apostle seemed to have believed the same thing:

Beloved, I pray that you may prosper in all things and be in health, just as your soul prospers (3 John 2).

How many millionaires have been born because of the Word of Faith teachings? How many businesses were started?

During the past 15 years, I've noticed an awakening in the body of Christ. It's an awakening to our role as believers and as ambassadors here on earth. We're not just trying to avoid sin so we can get to heaven with a better track record. We're not just trying to win as many souls to Jesus while our world is sinking deeper into moral oblivion. Could it be that our purpose as ambassadors is to infiltrate every level of society with the presence, power and principles of Christ? I believe that it is.

Take a moment to think about the many kingdoms that need salt and light. What about the local PTAs, city councils, unions, politics, sciences labs and soccer fields. What about the international think tanks or financial round tables? What about the great humanitarians and reformers that are needed for nations?

Let's become relevant again. Can we start to think differently about our children and grandchildren? After we get them ready for their eternal destiny, could we not equip, train and inspire them to think generationally? As a Christian from the 70s, I wasn't trained to think generationally. We all believed that Jesus was coming back any day.

I just celebrated my 55th birthday. Can I be honest with you? I never thought it would take that long for Jesus to return. If I'd been trained differently, I might've made a few different decisions that were more long term in nature. Now that my kids are married, I've changed my way of thinking. I'm now trying to prepare, help and train the next two generations to lead our Church movement for the next 50-100 years. If God grants me long life, I'd like to train the 3rd and 4th generations to buy real estate, become civic leaders, become doctors or lawyers and start businesses that can be passed on to their children and grandchildren. I feel like it's my responsibility to help position my children, grandchildren and great-grandchildren strategically to have a long term impact on society. We need more Spirit-filled scientists, writers, composers, billionaires, inventors, humanitarians and politicians. In my perspective, the next 20 to 30 years of my life should be dedicated to lifting up the Elijahs and Solomons that must impact the world with the power and principles of the Kingdom of heaven.

Denise and I have five incredible grandchildren with two more on the way. I never knew that my role in raising children would continue for a few more years. We're very involved in our grandchildren's lives. Soccer games, parties, babysitting and school plays are a blast. I consider it an honor to be so involved. The role of grandparents in the transfer of knowledge, anointing and resources cannot and should not be ignored.

Questions:
1) Did your parents and grandparents make decisions that were generational or short-sighted?
2) What about you? If Jesus returned today, would you be ready? What if He weren't returning for another 200 years? What ways would you think and believe differently?

11
THE KINGDOMS OF THIS WORLD

Then the seventh angel sounded: And there were loud voices in heaven, saying, "The kingdoms of this world have become the kingdoms of our Lord and of His Christ, and He shall reign forever and ever!" (Revelation 11:15)

As we discussed earlier, Dr. Lance Wallnau shared a truth that set our lives on a new course of understanding and application. Based upon a series of prophetic words and revelations from a man who died and returned back to life, Dr. Lance drew seven peaks that represented the seven kingdoms of this world. We're not talking about literal kingdoms, but the seven major areas that influence our world.

According to this model, the seven mountains are:

1. business/economy
2. family
3. government
4. education
5. media
6. arts & entertainment
7. religion

There's also an 8th mountain: the mountain of our God. It's His Kingdom that overlooks the others. It is, of course, the greatest of all, and one that is designed to expand. This is why Jesus prayed *Your Kingdom come. Your will be done.* As I mentioned earlier, I've modified my thinking and teachings in regards to the seven mountains. I've renamed it "The Keys of the Kingdom," and I speak about the many different types and sizes of kingdoms.

I know that the original approach was not meant to be an exclusive list of the mountains of this world. It helped me to make our approach even more relevant, to teach our congregation that there are very real principalities and powers that govern this world. People have built their kingdoms. As Christians, we're called to bring God's kingdom principles, ethics, morals and truths to every other kingdom in this world.

A great example of this truth in action is the work from members of our own congregation. In the past two years, we've seen many miracles, including two people raised from the dead and countless healings.

Three state laws have been changed to help stop sex trafficking in our state. And it all started with a few amazing people from our church who decided to tackle a horrible giant: the sex trade. For years, ICLV has had a measure of success helping girls escape that lifestyle. Some of them have become solid leaders in our church. We're so proud of them! It's been on my wife's heart for over ten years, and our women always opened their hearts to anyone stuck in prostitution.

But a more insidious element has continued to surface: *sex slavery.* Girls as young as twelve are being kidnapped, abused, raped, and then put into service as call girls. Pastor Steve, Aaron, Danita, Laura, Sarah-Jane, Kay and Esse are just a few of the people that have prayed, organized awareness conferences and networked with solid leaders from law enforcement in Las Vegas. The list is really too long to mention everyone, but you know who you are. May God bless you. These new laws will put the pimps in jail for a longer period of time and help make the way for trafficked slaves to be set free, helped and made whole.

Real Kingdoms, Real Ministries

As I traveled through Europe recently, I was shocked by the lack of borders between the members of the European Union. I couldn't help but remember my experience as a teenager living in Belgium. Every time I went to another country to play hockey or see the historic sites, I encountered checkpoints and border patrols.

Now they don't exist. This is the wave of the future—the borders between nations are coming down.

The real kingdoms that influence the whole earth are, in fact, borderless. Take, for example, the internet and TV. Those two mediums are causing widespread social upheavals in countries like India and China.

Media is able to cross over prohibited borders (like China), or social borders (like India), with a continual barrage of ideas that are in direct conflict with their country's ideology. Technology is changing in the world.

In Revelation 11:15, the voice from heaven exclaimed, *"The kingdoms of this world have become the kingdoms of our Lord and of His Christ, and He shall reign forever and ever!"* The kingdoms mentioned here are no longer referring to countries with kings, but with power centers that can change the course of history. Can you imagine every kingdom being dominated by Kingdom principles, laws and presence? Can you see God's incredible strategy? As the kingdoms gain more power, borders become more irrelevant. Those who occupy the power thrones will change the world.

Our services and ministry orientation have changed considerably since this revelation. As someone who carries an apostolic and pastoral mantle, I've encouraged, preached to, and taught men, women, teens and children to discover their God-given passion for science, music, the arts, business, drama, media, education, journalism, counseling, sports, law or whatever lights their fire.

God designed *you* to influence a kingdom within your city. Banking needs godly influencers; real-estate needs righteous men and women. Every industry needs Spirit-filled, anointed leaders to help create jobs, improve working conditions and impact society in a positive way. What lights your fire? Real ministry is not just from the pulpits of our churches. Real ministry should be happening in every boardroom, classroom, stadium, university and capital building.

Each one of us carries a heavenly assignment. We've been wired by God to accomplish the mission of transforming the kingdoms of this world. We aren't called to leave society, but to be the light within a dark society. How can we be a light if we remove ourselves from all "secular" enterprise? Who made them secular? Who placed that category on all that is not in the four walls of our churches?

As you discover your passion, you'll also get to know the gifts and talents that are dormant within you. You've been set up by God to be significant. God wants to reign over every area of influence and power, and He wants to do it through you.

Questions:
1) Are you ready to impact the kingdoms for God?
2) How will He use you to implement His strategy?
3) What do you have to offer the King to expand His Kingdom?

12
YOU'RE GIFTED. YOU'RE TALENTED.
YOU'RE FULLY EQUIPPED.

Key #6: God gives us gifts and talents to fulfill our mission

For the kingdom of heaven is like a man traveling to a far country, who called his own servants and delivered his goods to them. And to one he gave five talents, to another two, and to another one, to each according to his own ability; and immediately he went on a journey. Then he who had received the five talents went and traded with them, and made another five talents. And likewise he who had received two gained two more also. But he who had received one went and dug in the ground, and hid his lord's money. After a long time the lord of those servants came and settled accounts with them.

So he who had received five talents came and brought five other talents, saying, "Lord, you delivered to me five talents; look, I have gained five more talents besides them." His lord said to him, "Well done, good and faithful servant; you were faithful over a few things, I will make you ruler over many things. Enter into the joy of your lord" (Matthew 25:14-21).

Talents defined: "talanton"[1]— a balance, a certain weight (and thence a coin or rather sum of money) or "talent."

Ability defined: "dunamis"—force, specially, miraculous power.

You're called to discover what I call the "passion-DNA" that God placed in you before your birth. God also deposited more gifts and talents in you when you were born again and filled with His Spirit. Once you know your passion, you must then use the gifts and talents that God has placed in you through that same DNA.

For the kingdom of heaven is like…

Again, I love how Jesus started this parable. He used this illustration to teach His disciples how to bring Kingdom principles, power and presence into their daily lives. How could they establish the Kingdom without understanding it? The disciples needed to know all about the Kingdom, and they had to understand that they were given gifts and talents.

A talent reflects something that has value. Talents are given to every believer to help establish the Kingdom on earth.

Surprised By His Word

Let's take a closer look at the dunamis power of God.

And to one he gave five talents, to another two, and to another one, to each according to his own ability; and immediately he went on a journey (Matthew 25:15).

The Greek word for *ability* that Jesus used here surprised me. According to the scripture, God gave the talents based upon the *ability* which was already in them. In Acts 1:4, Jesus told His disciples to wait in Jerusalem until they received the dunamis (same Greek word) from heaven. In other words, God gives us talents, not based upon our good looks or good fortune, but based upon the amount of His power that we've already received from Him.

Wow! Are you getting this? Doesn't it make sense that we should desire more of God's power? When we receive more power, we receive more talents. Doesn't the Bible say that He is no respecter of persons? When God gives us stuff of value, He's being totally fair. Don't be jealous of those that have more talents than you. Just ask God to give you more power from on high. Then, get ready for a download of talents. James 4:1 is so clear in regards to asking God:

Where do wars and fights come from among you? Do they not come from your desires for pleasure that war in your members? You lust and do not have. You murder and covet and cannot obtain. You fight and war. Yet you do not have because you do not ask. You ask and do not receive, because you ask amiss, that you may spend it on your pleasures (James 4:1-3).

It's time to stop feeling sorry for ourselves. If you don't like what's going on in your life, then ask for His dunamis. If you don't like what you have, then ask God to fill you and change you. Then He'll be able to trust you with more. Ask God to forgive you for jealousy, envy or a victim mentality.

If you don't like what's going on in your school, government, business, neighborhood, or church, then ask God to help you change it. Don't wait for your good luck ship to come in. Swim out and grab it.

This is the message of the parable of talents. If we use what God has given us, He will reward us with much, much more. If we're filled with His power, we can be filled with more talents.

There are two ways to get more talents:
1. more dunamis
2. faithfulness

The Importance Of Faithfulness

It's impossible to bring the Kingdom of God to the earth without faithfulness.

We know that God is always faithful. The question is whether *you and I* will be. James 1:6-7 gives us the example of a double-minded man:

But let him ask in faith, with no doubting, for he who doubts is like a wave of the sea driven and tossed by the wind. For let not that man suppose that he will receive anything from the Lord; he is a double-minded man, unstable in all his ways.

The unfaithful man is double-minded. He shouldn't expect to receive *anything*. Are you faithful? If we're faithful, God will give us more authority to expand His Kingdom. Matthew 25:21 reveals this key:

His lord said to him, "Well done, good and faithful servant; you were faithful over a few things, I will make you ruler over many things. Enter into the joy of your lord."

Let's take a closer look at Jesus' words:
1. He called the servant "good and faithful." Can Jesus say the same about you?
2. What did the master mean when he said, "a few things"? This word translated as "few things" actually means *puny stuff* or *puny things.*

Things defined: "oligos"[2]—of uncertain affinity, puny, in extent, degree, number, duration or value.

Ruler defined: "kathistemi"[3]—to place down, to designate, constitute, convoy.

This reminds me of my wife, Denise. During Bible college, she cleaned toilets in the men's dorms. Many years later, she cleaned the church toilets. She even scrubbed our washrooms on Saturday nights to make sure they were done right.

Over the past few years, God has expanded Denise so much. My bride now leads a women's Bible study with five or six hundred in attendance every week. She speaks at conferences world-wide (and she's my favorite preacher). While I'm traveling, she leads ICLV. Denise is incredible.

Denise was faithful with puny stuff, now she rules over lots of stuff, and God's promoted her to greater authority. He's given this authority to her simply *because* she was faithful.

Big Promotions Are Coming Your Way

Important Step: Face Your Phobia

If we're faithful with little stuff, He will make us ruler (notice the use of this word) over much stuff. Wow, talk about a huge promotion. Let's tie this in with the Kingdom of heaven invading the kingdoms of this world. If we're faithful with the little things that God's given to us now, He'll make us ruler over businesses, churches, ministries, industries, schools, cities and states. My friend, Bishop Wellington Boone, preached a sermon at our church entitled "Total Domination."

I believe that this is God's desire for our lives. What are you waiting for? God wants to use you to bring His Kingdom down to this earth for His glory. Or, perhaps, you're like the servant who only received one talent? His excuse for not investing this one talent was fear. What's yours?

And I was afraid, and went and hid your talent in the ground. Look, there you have what is yours (Matthew 25:25).

Afraid defined: "phobeo"[4]—to frighten, to be alarmed, and to be in awe of, revere.

Fear caused the servant to conceal his talent; i.e., his value was being hidden because of fear. I've known a lot of Christians like this. They've been given so many wonderful gifts, talents and value from God, but they play it safe and allow fear to cripple them.

Did you know that the value of that one talent was actually a pretty substantial amount of money? One talent was equivalent to 6,000 denarii. One denarius was the wage for a normal day's work. In other words, this servant was given 6,000 days' worth of income. That works out to be over 16 years' worth of income. Wow! Take a moment and do the math. That's a lot of money. If you made $30,000 a year that would give you $480,000 in one lump sum. Someone say hallelujah, let it be done! I've known many people that didn't know the true value of their talent.

This servant was whining even though he was given almost a half million dollars. What a knucklehead! Oops, maybe some of us are guilty of this also. How many of us struggle with low self-esteem? How many of us struggle with fear and insecurity that stops us from going back to school, getting a better job or volunteering in our church? Don't you know who you are? Don't you know the valuable gifts that God has placed within you?

Then he who had received the one talent came and said, "Lord, I knew you to be a hard man, reaping where you have not sown, and gathering where you have not scattered seed" (Matthew 25:24).

This man had such a horrible view of God. He didn't see Him as a loving Father. My *Healthy Leaders* series goes into great detail about our view of God. Honestly, distorted views of God plague many church leaders and their congregations. This man with one talent saw Jesus as a cruel business owner. With this parable, Jesus introduced a new way of seeing God. He wanted us to know God like *He* knew God: like a father, like His Father.

Key #7: God concept
  Know God.
  Your view of God will determine your view of self. Change the way you see God and you'll change the way you see yourself.
  The master had given his servant almost a half million dollars to use, but he didn't use a penny. He had it all. Some of us have pretty bad views of God, "God doesn't love me! He doesn't care! He's not fair! He gave me cancer to teach me a lesson." There are so many examples of distorted God concepts. I've found that this is one of the biggest stumbling blocks to people reaching their potential. They have a distorted view of God. He is so good, but they don't see Him this way.
  Secondly, they have a distorted view of themselves. Every one of you is full of value, talents and blessings. Do you struggle with poor self-esteem? If you change the way you see God, it will change the way you see yourself. If you see yourself differently, you'll change your feelings, options, choices, actions and consequences. Changing your view of God will change how you interpret the events of your life.

Consider these scenarios:

Scenario I
Event:
> -*You were abused as a child*

Distorted View of God:
> -*He doesn't care, He loves to punish us*

Interpretation:
> -*God allowed it to happen to teach me a lesson*
> -*God didn't protect me because I wasn't perfect*
> -*God was punishing me*
> -*God doesn't love me; otherwise, He would've stopped the abuse from happening*

Feelings:
> -*I'm angry with God*
> -*I'm worthless*
> -*I don't feel loved*

Long-term effects:
> -*Poor self-esteem*
> -*Victim or abuse mentality*
> -*Unable to see healthy options*

Scenario II
Event:
> -*You were abused as a child*

Right View of God:
> -*God loves me*
> -*He hated what happened to me*
> -*He only allowed it because He gave everyone a free will*

Interpretation:
> -*My abuser is 100% responsible*
> -*God gave that person free will; he/she chose to use it to harm me*
> -*God is my best friend*
> -*God is the One that wants to heal me*
> -*God wants to take my tragedies and turn them into triumph*

Feelings:
> -*I feel healed, loved, empowered and wiser*

Long-term effects:
-I get closer to God
-I forgive my abuser
-I help prevent abuse in others
-I help other victims of abuse
-I have a healthy relationship with God and others

Isn't this one truth life changing? The way you see God will affect how you interpret the trials, tragedies and joys of life.

The Apostle Paul experienced many horrible trials and persecutions and, yet, He had an incredible outlook on life. He said of God,

Now to Him who is able to do exceedingly abundantly above all that we ask or think, according to the power that works in us (Ephesians 3:20).

He said of himself,

I can do all things through Christ who strengthens me (Philippians 4:13).

Because he saw Jesus clearly, he was able to see his own value clearly. If you see your value clearly, you'll naturally invest it wisely. Someone once said that life is not about owning; it's about stewardship. God has fully equipped you and me with gifts, talents and eternal value. You are a person of great value and giftedness. What are you doing with it?

Change The Way You See Yourself

Is it God's will for you to:

1. see Him clearly?
2. recognize your value and talents?
3. dedicate yourself to God's design?

This book is dedicated to helping you answer these questions with absolute surety.

Jesus said, "But seek first the Kingdom of God and His righteousness, and all these things shall be added to you" (Matthew 6:33).

If you use your gifts, talents, energy and passion for bringing the Kingdom of heaven to the kingdoms of this world, all this stuff will be added to you. Most people chase after stuff. God's people should seek first His Kingdom and to forgive and be free, having right standing with God. If you're faithful with what He has already given you, He will make you ruler over many things. I know that you must be asking yourself, "But how, God?

How can I become a ruler?" Peter must have asked himself the same thing when Jesus offered him the keys of the Kingdom.

A beautiful example of this reality is the life of my friends, Pasqual and Norma.

Many years ago, Norma attended the small chapel that we had just completed on 15 acres in Las Vegas. It was a big step for our little church, but God showed up in a significant way. The Church started growing, and people were experiencing the presence of God. So many lives were being changed. It was and still is amazing at ICLV.

During a powerful service, Norma responded to an altar call. She did so almost every week for a while. She would fall to her knees and just cry and cry. But this particular service was different. As she fell to her knees, I had a thought in my mind: her husband will be saved this year. I frankly didn't even know that she was married. I hesitated for a moment, then truly felt that I had received a word of knowledge from God. So I walked over to her and declared, "Your husband will be saved this year." Norma cried even more.

Just a few months later, Pasqual came to The Lord. A crack addict and a third degree black belt, gang influence and violence were common in his life. But Jesus captured his soul, and we began to train him, heal him and love him.

One day, many moons later, I felt led to ask Pasqual to travel with me around the world. I was traveling to some pretty dangerous places at the time, and it seemed good to me to bring a friend who could defend himself. I must admit that he saved me on more than one occasion. We've become amazing friends and team members. This year, God has taken this man from a minister on the mean streets of Las Vegas to the immigration debates in Washington, DC. His voice and influence are extending on a national level. He's been promoted by God to influence immigration in the US. *Incredible, isn't it?*

Pasqual and Norma are just two of the many in our church and ministry that see themselves in new light. You can begin this wonderful journey, too. I believe that you are an Elisha in waiting.

Exercise:
Make a list of five decrees about who you are in Jesus Christ. For example, I am valuable, lovable, talented, gifted, and anointed.

Questions:
1) Do you want the keys of the Kingdom?
2) Are you ready to use the keys for His honor and glory?
3) Do you see God clearly or do you need to pray for a new God concept

ENDNOTES

1. *Talanton*, NT: Strong's #5007

2. *Oligos*, NT: Strong's #3641

3. *Kathistemi*, NT: Strong's #2525

4. *Phobeo*, NT: Strong's #5399

13
THE KEYS OF THE KINGDOM
ARE GIVEN TO YOU

And I also say to you that you are Peter, and on this rock I will build My church, and the gates of Hades shall not prevail against it. And I will give you the keys of the kingdom of heaven, and whatever you bind on earth will be bound in heaven, and whatever you loose on earth will be loosed in heaven (Matthew 16:18-19).

Wow, this must have seemed so overwhelming to Peter. Have you ever received a prophetic word that sounded so huge it made you feel puny? I can relate to how Peter must have felt when he received this huge word; namely, overwhelmed, confused, proud and intimidated. I personally believe that this promise of keys and huge authority was not only meant for Peter, but for everyone who makes the same confession. As I studied this scripture, I discovered what I like to call "The 7 Gems," which can be applied to our own lives and ministries. Check it out.

The 7 Gems In Matthew 16

As a result of Peter's powerful realization and confession:

1. Jesus blessed him. Jesus always blesses us when we get it right.
2. Jesus used his full name, Simon Bar-Jonah; perhaps He didn't want anyone else to grab the blessing (just kidding). All of us love it when someone calls us by our full name.
3. He witnessed to the source of Peter's revelation—the Father told him. Wow! Peter was tapped into the Father just like Jesus had been tapped into Him.
4. Jesus changed his name to Peter. Revelation transforms our identity.
5. Peter defined: "Petros"1—A piece of rock, as a name, Petrus, an apostle.
6. Jesus prophesied that He would build His Church on this confession. In one sentence, Jesus revealed His true focus: I will build my Church.
7. Even the devil in hell couldn't defeat the Church that Jesus will build. The Church is the King's way of advancing His Kingdom in this world.

The battlefield for the kingdoms is at the gates of hell. This is why God plants you and me in tough places. We're not supposed to hide out in little heavenly incubators. Although there's nothing wrong with finding our intimate places with Jesus, we're all called to confront the enemy's strongholds, even up to the gates of hell.

Charities and businesses can fail, but the Church that Jesus is building can never fail.

In order for Peter to fulfill his new leadership position, Jesus gave him the keys to His home—the keys to bring the Kingdom of heaven to this earth.

When Denise and I arrived in Las Vegas, we were completely overwhelmed and unprepared. Las Vegas is the only city in the world called "sin city." It's our mission to change that name. Vegas isn't an easy place, but that's exactly why Jesus sent us here.

We've Got The Keys

A few years ago, Denise and I had a home built. We were so anxious to move in. We got all packed and loaded into a moving truck, but were unable to move in because the funding and documents weren't finalized. Although I pleaded for the keys, the builders wouldn't give them to me until funding had arrived and ownership was clearly established.

What did Peter think when he heard those words, *"I will give you the keys of the kingdom"*? Wow! A million thoughts must have shot through his mind, like, "What keys?" "When will I get these keys and how do I use them?" Peter was given a glimpse of the authority that was about to be his. I'm sure he didn't know what the keys were, but he soon found out. God has always wanted to reveal His mysteries to His children. Peter had a vision that opened the door to Gentile converts. Paul had a dream of a man from Macedonia calling for his help. Mysteries are part of life, but the Holy Spirit wants to reveal them to us.

...to know the love of Christ which passes knowledge; that you may be filled with all the fullness of God (Ephesians 3:19).

God wants to reveal His deep mysteries to you. Because God is your Father, He wants to tell you all the family secrets. Jesus, our Master, has opened the door for us to access the Father. He wants to hand you the keys to blessing, joy, peace, health, prosperity, purpose and, especially, the keys of the family Kingdom. These keys are universal; they're powerful; and they're meant to be used.

ENDNOTES

1. *Peter*, NT: Strong's #4074

14
THE GRACE OF GOD IS GIVEN TO YOU

Key #8: Grace

> *For by grace you have been saved through faith, and that not of yourselves; it is the gift of God, not of works, lest anyone should boast. For we are His workmanship, created in Christ Jesus for good works, which God prepared beforehand that we should walk in them (Ephesians 2:8-10).*

Without God's grace, we could never even be worth a glass of water; but He has made us worthy of all blessings and honor:

> *For He made Him who knew no sin to be sin for us, that we might become the righteousness of God in Him (2 Corinthians 5:21).*

We have become the righteousness of God. Wow. We're now worthy to represent the Father. The Bible even calls us co-heirs with Christ:

> *If children, then heirs—heirs of God and joint heirs with Christ, if indeed we suffer with Him, that we may also be glorified together (Romans 8:17).*

Paul had a full grasp of his unworthiness and the grace of God that made him worthy. You and I may be full of personal weaknesses and faults, but we're still worthy heirs because of Jesus Christ and *His* great work. That's why Jesus said, *"It is finished,"* on the cross. *Mission accomplished.*

To me, who am less than the least of all the saints, this grace was given, that I should preach among the Gentiles the unsearchable riches of Christ, and to make all see what is the fellowship of the mystery, which from the beginning of the ages has been hidden in God who created all things through Jesus Christ (Ephesians 3:8-9).

We've been forgiven—our sins are in the sea of forgetfulness. We've been made heirs of God and joint heirs with Jesus Christ. The fact that God wants to use us isn't based on our own perfection but the perfection of Christ and His sacrifice for us. We're covered with the blood of Christ, which makes us righteous in God's sight.

...how much more shall the blood of Christ, who through the eternal Spirit offered Himself without spot to God, cleanse your conscience from dead works to serve the living God? And for this reason He is the Mediator of the new covenant, by means of death, for the redemption of the transgressions under the first covenant, that those who are called may receive the promise of the eternal inheritance (Hebrews 9:14-15).

If we understand this key, it will release us from a guilty conscience and the accusations of the devil. It will also guard us against pride. Christians should never struggle with insecurity; we should struggle with pride, because God has elevated us to such an incredible height:

...and [Jesus Christ] has made us kings and priests to His God and Father, to Him be glory and dominion forever and ever. Amen (Revelation 1:6).

Never forget that grace takes care of all your sins and weaknesses, past, present and future. God knows that you are not perfect; nevertheless, He wants to use you to influence and conquer new territory for Him.

His Message Is Given To Us

And as you go, preach, saying, "The kingdom of heaven is at hand" (Matthew 10:7).

Remember that this message is your first key: *the Kingdom within you is greater than the kingdom of this world.*

The message that God has given to us is a key to unlock the hearts of men and women. The Kingdom of heaven is at hand...why? Good question. Because everywhere you go you bring it.

...nor will they say, 'See here!' or 'See there!' For indeed, the Kingdom of God is within you (Luke 17:21).

And wherever you go you bring His rule. Why? Because the Kingdom living inside you, by His Spirit, overrules the principalities of this world. Wow! That's what the seventy disciples discovered in Luke. They discovered that the Kingdom of God was upon them, and that the Kingdom *within* them was more powerful than earthly kingdoms:

Then the seventy returned with joy, saying, "Lord, even the demons are subject to us in Your name" (Luke 10:17).

Their initial mission was to heal the sick and tell people that the Kingdom was near. A simple task, isn't it? Was their mission accomplished? Absolutely! Plus, they discovered their authority over demonic powers and diseases.

Why were the healings important? Because they demonstrated that these seventy had something from another place. They had power to destroy sickness in bodies. The power that the disciples received from Jesus was greater than the sickness and disease that crippled people's lives. Even demons were subject to them in His name.

Can you imagine their surprise? They could heal the sick and cast out demonic powers. Amazing. All of this proved the veracity of their announcement: *the Kingdom is near.* It was one message backed with the power to substantiate it.

Why was the message important? Because it revealed that God's desire was to bring His Kingdom into their homes, businesses, relationships and even their own bodies. The healings were a foretaste of a heavenly reality.

The message also spoke of the King that was coming to their town. Jesus was the coming King.

When you and I walk into a room, we change the laws that govern that environment. The King within us helps us to usher in a new atmosphere. This is why it says,

You are of God, little children, and have overcome them, because He who is in you is greater than he who is in the world (1 John 4:4).

Because Jesus is in your body, mind and spirit, you bring the Kingdom of heaven everywhere you go. The King that is in you is greater than the one that is temporarily running the world.

Don't forget that behind the kingdoms of this world lies a deceiver—the prince of the power of the air. He governs principalities and powers that are unseen; invisible groves that are dedicated to stealing, killing and destroying.

When the seventy returned, Jesus underlined the success of their foray: *"I saw satan fall like lightning."* In other words, "Good job guys. I saw satan being dethroned from the high places because of your actions."

Paul also illustrated this principle when he referred to our lives being like perfume:

Now thanks be to God who always leads us in triumph in Christ, and through us diffuses the fragrance of His knowledge in every place. For we are to God the fragrance of Christ among those who are being saved and among those who are perishing (2 Corinthians 2:14-15).

Perfume penetrates the oxygen in a room. The more perfume, the more people smell it. We are called to release a beautiful scent of heaven into eerie, foul environments.

Did you know that you've been called a living epistle?

You are our epistle written in our hearts, known and read by all men; clearly you are an epistle of Christ, ministered by us, written not with ink but by the Spirit of the living God, not on tablets of stone but on tablets of flesh, that is, of the heart (2 Corinthians 3:2-3).

You are a living epistle. The end is not here yet. Our obedience to the Spirit will fill up volumes of good works being recorded in heaven.

The Word Of God Is Powerful

Your decisions, words and actions are a message to the world that Christ is your King. As 21st century Christians, we've been blessed with access to the message in writing. It's called the Word of God. We live in a day when the resources that help us study and understand His Word are readily available. This Word should be in all of our minds and hearts, *"For the word of God is living and powerful, and sharper than any two-edged sword, piercing even to the division of soul and spirit, and of joints and marrow, and is a discerner of the thoughts and intents of the heart"* (Hebrews 4:12). God promised that this living and active Word will never return void:

So shall My word be that goes forth from My mouth; It shall not return to Me void but it shall accomplish what I please, and it shall prosper in the thing for which I sent it (Isaiah 55:11).

Every time you read, study or share it, the Word of God will bear fruit. Every time you speak the Word over your life, family, career, church, city, or nation, it will have a dynamic effect. When the prophet Ezekiel spoke over the valley of dry bones, life came back to the skeletal remains:

Again He said to me, "Prophesy to these bones, and say to them, 'O dry bones, hear the word of the LORD! Thus says the Lord GOD to these bones: "Surely I will cause breath to enter into you, and you shall live. I will put sinews on you and bring flesh upon you, cover you with skin and put breath in you; and you shall live. Then you shall know that I am the LORD""" (Ezekiel 37:4-6).

In the same manner, God wants us to speak over the dead bones of our past failures and defeats. The Bible reassures us, *"Yet in all these things we are more than conquerors through Him who loved us"* (Romans 8:37).

Conquerors can face the enemy and defeat him. Once the enemy is defeated, it's time to claim the spoils of victory and take new territory for God. We should be advancing God's Kingdom and His Church in every home and office in America. If we're faithful with this responsibility, He'll give us nations.

Ask of Me, and I will give You the nations for Your inheritance, and the ends of the earth for Your possession (Psalm 2:8).

When we built our main sanctuary, we had Psalm 2:8 molded into the cement walls. Today you can still find it at the front entrance. We've declared it over our ministry. It's not a coincidence that I've had the privilege of ministering in over 40 countries. Team members have extended our Kingdom influence to the world by the power of the Holy Spirit. It's been exciting to see ICLV impact nations.

Our message is all about Christ and His Kingdom. It will cover every city and nation of our world,

...that at the name of Jesus every knee should bow, of those in heaven, and of those on earth, and of those under the earth, and that every tongue should confess that Jesus Christ is Lord, to the glory of God the Father (Philippians 2:10-11).

I'm amazed at the way God has used us. He's given us the ability to touch nations. If you want to check out some of these miracles just go to our website at www.ICLV.com.

One tremendous example comes immediately to mind. About a dozen years ago, I was invited to minister in India. I didn't know what to expect when I landed in Delhi. Frankly, I overwhelmed by the sights, sounds and smells. Our small team ministered in slums, houses, churches, even on a rooftop. It was insane how God used us. One of the strategies that God has given us is to find the Elishas and Timothies. When we find them, we invest in them in every possible way. We pour; we give; we model and we work side by side.

In Romans 1:11, Paul revealed this same approach. We learned it from him, of course!

> *For I long to see you, that I may impart to you some spiritual gift, so that you may be established.*

He longed to see the Roman believers so that he could impart to them spiritual gifts. The word *impart* is unique. It's translated from the Greek word "metadidomi," which means that Paul had *many gifts* that he wanted to transfer. This wasn't a new principle. Elisha asked for a double portion of Elijah's spirit, and Joshua had a spirit of wisdom because Moses laid hands on him.

Once you realize that God has called, empowered, anointed and prepared you to bring His Kingdom to the kingdoms of this world, the Lord will give you nations. You'll have the confidence to pour into others, who can then claim their own territory.

On this first trip, we met just such a man. He had a small church of about fifty, but I saw something in him. We ministered together and he followed me. He helped us so much, and we poured into him and his little band of volunteers. I'm thrilled to announce that Ivan and Nini have around 6,000 people in their church now, and they've started many dynamic ministries of compassion and power. Their slum schools teach, feed, clothe and minister to over 1900 kids daily. If it weren't for Ivan and his team, most of these kids would have died, been caught up in gangs, sold into prostitution, or some other atrocity.

God has given Ivan and Nini the keys to northern India. I feel so honored and humbled to work with people like them.

15
THE FIVE POWERS OF GOD

And He said to them, "I saw satan fall like lightning from heaven. Behold, I give you the authority to trample on serpents and scorpions, and over all the power of the enemy, and nothing shall by any means hurt you" (Luke 10:18-19).

The powers of God make up our second key. Although we mentioned them earlier, I wanted to highlight them again to unwrap these gifts from God in more detail.

Some of you have heard teachings on the true meaning of the word "love" in the New Testament. Every time we come across this word in the New Testament, we should ask ourselves which Greek word was used by the author. Oftentimes, our English translation fails to reflect the fullness of the author's intent. There are actually four words in the Greek that are translated as "love."

The four words for love are:
- Agape—*unconditional love*
- Phileo—*brotherly love*
- Storge—*family love*
- Eros—*emotional love*

The same problem occurs with the word "power." There are actually five Greek words commonly translated as "power." If you read the New Testament exclusively in English, you're probably missing the original meaning of the passage. A thorough examination of all five Greek words and their meaning can be found in my book, *The 5 Powers of God*. These powers represent a whole set of keys for bringing the Kingdom into your world. Let's take a closer look at them.

Dunamis[1]
force, specially, miraculous power

> *But you shall receive power [dunamis] when the Holy Spirit has come upon you; and you shall be witnesses to Me in Jerusalem, and in all Judea and Samaria, and to the end of the earth (Acts 1:8).*

This word and its derivatives are used over 100 times in the New Testament. I guess it must be pretty important. In the Luke 10:19 passage, we're told that even satan has power, but our authority exceeds his.

When we pray for the sick, this is the type of power we need to flow either through us or directly to the suffering person. It's explosive....*dynamite!*

When people are seeking the baptism of the Holy Spirit, I pray that God will fill them with dunamis. In Acts 1, Jesus told the disciples that after they were filled with dunamis, they would evangelize the world. That's pretty impressive, isn't it?

Exousia[2]
privilege, force, capacity, competency, freedom, or mastery (concretely, magistrate, super human, potentate, token of control), delegated influence

> *Behold, I give you the authority [exousia] to trample on serpents and scorpions, and over all the power of the enemy, and nothing shall by any means hurt you (Luke 10:19).*

Exousia is often translated as *authority* or *power*. Authority is more accurate. In the Luke passage, the disciples are given authority over all of the dunamis of the enemy. Praise God! He gave us authority over all of the devil's dunamis. Although I've already talked about authority as one of the powers of God, I feel that it deserves more attention. It's way too important.

In many translations, the word has been improperly translated. Exousia is used over 100 times in the New Testament. I guess God wants us to understand it. Ironically, many churches build doctrines that ignore or deny the principle of spiritual authority based on one or two isolated scriptures, but this revelation is mentioned throughout the New Testament.

We need exousia in the boardrooms of businesses, in colleges and government halls. It will bring you confidence. When you receive authority, fear no longer hinders you. You won't fear man when the authority of God fills you and flows through you. Over the past ten years, I've had the privilege of praying for countless people to receive one or all of the five powers of God. It's been a blast to see people come back with reports of huge breakthroughs, especially in regards to the power of exousia. Parents, business leaders, pastors and athletes have all testified to the remarkable difference it's made in their lives.

Energeia[3] (energeo)
efficiency ("energy")

This term is used over 30 times in the New Testament. Energeia is the root word for our English words *energy* or *energetic*. How many times have you needed energy in your ventures or responsibilities? God wants to give this energy to you.

The mother of young kids needs energy; the single parent holding down two jobs needs energy. The energy drink industry is skyrocketing; perhaps everyone needs more energy.

Kratos[4]
dominion, might, power, strength

This word is used less frequently in the Bible, but it's still available to each one of us. Kratos signifies the *dominion* that Christ the King wants to exercise through you and me. This entire book has highlighted God's desire to bring the Kingdom of God to the kingdoms of this earth. He wants to do it through you.

Kratos power will help you establish the Kingdom more every day. It helps you to increase in influence. Daniel increased in influence while in captivity. Joseph increased in influence while a slave. Kratos supernaturally helps you to rise in favor and influence. I've seen this in our church and my own life. It's truly insane.

Consider my friend John. He got out of prison three-and-half years ago. While in prison, he had an encounter with Christ. God even gave him a vision of a future ministry. It seemed impossible, but God did a great thing through him and his family.

Another friend of ours, Jeremiah, along with others, joined in the effort to train men and women in leadership upon their release from prison. It's common knowledge that many ex-prisoners reoffend shortly after their release. God gave John the kratos and wisdom to crack the code for this problem. They've had a 70% success rate in training these individuals and helping them find jobs. *Amazing!* John has had the recognition of city and state officials. His program for the reintegration of these ex-convicts will be introduced to fifty mayors in a few months. The kratos is working. It could go national!

God, pour out Your kratos power through every one of us, we pray.

Ischus[5]
force, ability, strength

Have you ever needed more strength in your life? Just ask God for it. Ask for the strength to confront challenges and to resist temptations. We all need a dose of God's strength. Weariness is a common occurrence in ministry, especially in our busy culture. The Word exhorts us:

> *And let us not grow weary while doing good, for in due season we shall reap if we do not lose heart (Galatians 6:9).*

The ischus of God helps us to keep from growing weary. I'm 55 years old. My schedule is hectic. My travel itinerary is taxing. So I pray for ischus strength…a lot.

We also need strength to resist temptation and to fight discouragement. Do you need strength?

> *The thief does not come except to steal, and to kill, and to destroy. I have come that they may have life, and that they may have it more abundantly (John 10:10).*

These five powers are designed to enable Christians to have the same vibrant, abundant life that Jesus had. They help us to accomplish our divine assignment, which is to unlock heaven and release it into the world.

A vibrant life finds its fulfillment in doing what God intended for us to do. The powers of God are gifts to help us defeat giants in the land, bring down demonic strongholds and bring His Kingdom into every kingdom of this world.

Do you remember how surprised the disciples were when even demons were subject to them?

> *Then the seventy returned with joy, saying, "Lord, even the demons are subject to us in Your name" (Luke 10:17).*

Subject defined: "hupotasso"[6]—to subordinate, reflexively, to obey.

The word "subject" means *in submission*. The disciples realized that when they took authority in Jesus' name to heal the sick and spread the message of the Kingdom, even demons had to be submissive to them.

As the disciples used the authority which Jesus imparted[7] to them, they dispossessed demonic power wherever they went. God knows which powers you need to defeat the enemy in your life or city. Not only does He know which ones, but He wants to give them to you.

In the next chapter, let me show you a few examples.

ENDNOTES

1. *Dunamis*, NT: Strong's #1411

2. *Exousia*, NT: Strong's #1849

3. *Energeia*, NT: Strong's #1756

4. *Kratos*, NT: Strong's #2904

5. *Ischus*, NT: Strong's #2479

6. *Hupotasso*, NT: Strong's #5293

7. See my book, *The Power of Impartation*, to learn and understand impartation.

16
REAL-LIFE STORIES OF
THE FIVE POWERS IN ACTION

Dunamis: Miracle Working Power

ICLV's mission team has been to many countries around the world. One area in which we've needed to display the dunamis of God is India. We've seen thousands touched by God's power: blind eyes and deaf ears opened, the lame walking, and many diseases healed in the name of Jesus. Our work there has exploded. And we've seen these demonstrations of power in our meetings around the world. The altars are full of people getting healed, saved and set free, all due to God's power flowing through us.

But don't forget that this distribution of power isn't limited to *dynamite* dunamis. Every situation requires wisdom. Every situation requires discernment. Every situation does *not* require dunamis.

Sometimes, people need a display of authority.

Exousia: Authority

I've taught our people at ICLV that God wants to give them the five powers. We can ask for His power, but He will decide which one(s) we need to accomplish His assignments.

During an altar call a few years ago, I saw my 16-year-old son, Samuel, come to the altar asking for God's power. He didn't seem emotional at all; he simply stood there waiting. As we drove home together, I asked him what he'd received from God. He quickly responded, "Authority, dad."

As the youngest basketball player on a state championship team, Samuel asked for a divine impartation of exousia so that he could excel and help his team win. In only a few weeks, it was amazing to see his progress.

After an important game, one of his coaches approached me in the parking lot to ask, "What happened to your son?"

Praise God! His coach saw that something had changed in Samuel. It was so exciting to see him contribute to his team at the state semifinals and finals. Samuel didn't need dunamis for those games. He didn't need to fall out in the Spirit or speak in tongues. He didn't need to heal the sick or cast out devils. If any of this had happened, he would've been quite out of place. God wants to give you *what you need* in each circumstance. Samuel received the type of power that would help him excel for the glory of God.

For far too many years, evangelicals have been afraid to ask God for His power in fear, perhaps, that somebody might speak in tongues or react strangely during a service. Pentecostals, on the other hand, seem to have limited God's power to an emotional reaction, or manifestations such as tongues, shaking, laughing, falling, or crying. But is it possible that God can download the gift of authority without us *feeling* anything?

In the Luke 10 passage, we didn't see the disciples fall out as they received more authority. In fact, the only one that got really emotional was Jesus:

> *In that hour Jesus rejoiced in the Spirit and said, "I thank You, Father, Lord of heaven and earth, that You have hidden these things from the wise and prudent and revealed them to babes. Even so, Father, for so it seemed good in Your sight" (Luke 10:21).*

The Greek word used here for "rejoiced" indicates that Jesus began jumping and spinning as He talked to His Daddy about His followers. I think this is totally cool. He was thrilled that the seventy had successfully defeated satan in another region. Remember, He said, *"I saw satan fall..." (Luke 10:17)*

> *Behold, I give you the authority [exousia] to trample on serpents and scorpions, and over all the power of the enemy (Luke 10:19).*

Jesus was excited that the leadership team had grown from 12 to 82, and that they all applied His message and power with impressive results.

I think He still feels excited when we grab the same keys and rev the engines for the glory of God. Because they were faithful with the first impartation, He gave them a second one. He rewarded the seventy with authority over *all* of the devil's power. Praise God!

Can you imagine a businessman who asks God for His power before a big presentation? Wouldn't he look silly in front of the board members if he spoke in tongues? That's not the type of power that he needs. He needs authority power. He needs to walk in there with confidence, passion and a clear mind. Every demonic stronghold in the place will have to move aside for the man of God to speak.

The powers of God are not just designed for church services. They're designed for every believer to use in every place they go to spread the presence of the King everywhere—praise God!

You Will Stand Before Kings

Do you see a man who excels in his work? He will stand before kings; He will not stand before unknown men (Proverbs 22:29).

I'll never forget a presidential luncheon that I was invited to by a friend. I'd always wanted to meet President Bush in person, but never had the chance. I know that his eight-year tenure as president was marked with some pretty big successes, and some questionable decisions. I don't envy the role of any president. They need our prayers more than ever.

Nevertheless, I jumped at the opportunity to hear him live and in-person. After dinner, my three friends and I rushed to the front to shake the president's hand. Wow, I was rocked by his message of vision and authenticity. I mentioned to one of the organizers my excitement and invited the president to Las Vegas to share his vision.

Now, please hear my heart. I'm just a normal person, but I believe that God can do extraordinary things through me and my family, friends and church. The invitation came from my heart and spirit. Something he said resonated in me. The chances of a president coming to Vegas because of my invitation seemed pretty slim.

To my surprise, the next day while I was playing golf, I received a phone call from a political leader. At first I thought it was a joke, but I realized that he was serious when he said, "The president has decided to accept your invitation." They wanted *my* help to make this type of event happen in my city of Las Vegas.

At the end of our conversation, I had a confession to make that was troubling me. I said, "Sir, I must admit that I'm not a US citizen yet, but I have a green card." I'm sure I sounded pretty silly, but it goes to show that the authority God gave me to invite the president was real and powerful. As a private citizen, I had the privilege of playing a very small part in the dinner, but it was so exciting.

Towards the end, I brought my little family up to meet President Bush. What a tremendous honor! When President Bush shook my son's hand, he leaned up close to his face and said, "Your father is a great man."

He really doesn't know me. Why would he say such a thing? Could it be that he identified the great one that resides in me? I'm not ashamed of the One that lives in me. He is my King. I serve His Kingdom. My deepest desire is to expand His influence in every sphere of power and influence, in every dark place, in every broken life. This is our destiny.

The Bible says, *"Remind them to be subject to rulers and authorities, to obey, to be ready for every good work" (Titus 3:1).* God has given our leaders at ICLV great authority in the political realm.

As a missionary to the USA, I've fallen in love with this great country. God is still saying, *"Ask of Me, and I will give You the nations for Your inheritance" (Psalm 2:8).* In our main sanctuary, we have many flags from the nations of the world hanging from our rafters. We pray continually for God to use us locally, nationally and globally.

Ask God for more exousia. It can and will affect your career, family, finances and your nation. If God can use an old French Canadian transplant to bless national leaders, God can use you.

Energeia: Energy

Have you ever heard someone who's entrenched in New Age beliefs talk about the "energy" that surrounds you? It strikes me as humorous when someone says they see an "aura" around me, or that they "feel my energy." When they say these things I simply agree with them. Generally, I'll respond, "Yes, I know." Then I'll let them know that the source of the energy is the Holy Spirit.

I was recently finalizing a purchase when one of the salespeople turned in surprise and said, "Did you feel that? "

He looked at the other sales people, wondering where the source of energy was coming from. I just smiled and told him I felt it too. He didn't know that I was standing there asking God for His favor and leaning into His wonderful Spirit.

Christian people should feel the energy of God when they stand close to you, and you should feel it when it leaves your body. Jesus felt it when the faith of the woman with the issue of blood drained power out of His body.

Immediately the fountain of her blood was dried up, and she felt in her body that she was healed of the affliction. And Jesus, immediately knowing in Himself that power had gone out of Him, turned around in the crowd and said, "Who touched My clothes?" (Mark 5:29-30).

While a young Christian, I was trained to base my faith on the Word, not on emotions. That was great advice that I have lived with and taught.

There is, however, another side to this truth. Although we don't base our faith and decisions on feelings, we need to be sensitive to the move of the Holy Spirit and God's release of power. I don't always need to feel God, but it's great when I do.

Paul sensed this urgency when he said, *"...that I may know Him and the power of His resurrection, and the fellowship of His sufferings, being conformed to His death" (Philippians 3:10).*

Know defined: "ginosko"[1]— to "know" (absolutely) in a great variety of applications and with many implications.

The word for "know" means *to be intimate with*. Paul wanted to *intimately* know the dunamis of the resurrection.[2] Wow. His desire was to tap into the 220 volts from heaven. He wanted to experience it, understand it and release it into the lives of others.

Why would God send energy into our lives? Just ask a single mother if she would like more energy. Ask the man working two jobs if he needs more energy. Have you recently noticed the use of energy drinks and energy bars? Have you ever noticed how many people drink coffee for a little boost? What about the couple with a handicapped child or an aging parent? They need energy like we all need water. Do you have five kids and a truck load of laundry? Ask God for energeia!

About eight years ago, John Maxwell asked me for a favor. That sounds intimidating doesn't it? The "godfather" of leadership was asking me for help. I immediately said yes. Without thinking or praying or getting more facts, I just said, "sure."

You see, I owed John Maxwell. I'd been reading his books for years. They helped me so much. He'd also helped us raise funds for our large sanctuary. He'd poured into our leaders. I was so grateful for his life. As our discussion progressed on the golf course, he explained that he had a vision to train one million leaders with a new curriculum he'd just finished. He already had associate trainers in other languages, but lacked someone who could speak French.

Now this is where it got stressful. I'd said yes before I knew he wanted me to speak French. Although my roots are French Canadian, I had given up speaking French fluently. I only spoke French when I had to, and only with great frustration and insecurity.

Have you ever said yes to something but later regretted it? Yeah, that was me.

It's funny, because I'd already received three prophetic words that I was supposed to help the French. Years prior, Bill Bright had even prayed with me and started crying, urging me to go to France. I have to admit, I really had to think twice about this one. Denial becomes an effective device when you're afraid!

I've been going to France for over eight years now. It's been one of the most rewarding things I've ever done. Serving EQUIP by training French leaders worldwide has been, and continues to be, a huge honor. The results have been unbelievable. Paris, Dijon, Switzerland, Quebec, Martinique, Marseille and many African countries are being trained in godly leadership. The fruits of these relationships and trainings have been glorious. The Churches are growing, families are becoming healthier and cities are being influenced.

Kratos: Dominion

Kratos power is needed any time we face demonic resistance. Our battle is not against flesh and blood. (Ephesians 6:12) We should establish and extend the dominion of Christ into every situation.

Kratos is a requirement for spiritual warfare. It's needed by moms and dads to lead their families, as well as businessmen for the advancement of their visions. Kratos always establishes Christ as King in every setting. It's *His* dominion that we're extending, not our own personal agenda. Kratos power helps us to spread the dominion of God's Kingdom on the earth.

It's been so inspiring to see over five state laws changed due to team members from ICLV; to see prisoners trained and helped to secure jobs; to see lives changed for the glory of God.

Ischus: Strength

Ischus is strength from above. Joshua needed strength to enter the Promised Land.

> *Have I not commanded you? Be strong and of good courage; do not be afraid, nor be dismayed, for the LORD your God is with you wherever you go (Joshua 1:9).*

We need strength to overcome addiction, temptation and opposition. In James 5:16, we're told that our prayers are strong. James realized that he had more ischus as God helped him to overcome weaknesses, *"Confess your trespasses to one another, and pray for one another, that you may be healed. The effective, fervent prayer of a righteous man avails much."*

My wife and I needed strength when our eldest daughter, Isabelle, was diagnosed with cancer. As I look back, I realize that my strength was made perfect by God's power. Isabelle's strength was unbelievable. To be honest with you, my wife had more strength than I had during this serious trial. The miracle of Isabelle's healing is just one aspect of the download of strength we got from the Lord.

As our church staff has grown from 5 to over 160, I've needed God's strength. As we've purchased five properties in Las Vegas to expand around the city, I've cried out for God's strength. Paul understood this need just like the rest of us. When life hits us hard with the loss of loved ones or various setbacks, we all need ischus.

Finally, my brethren, be strong in the Lord and in the power of His might. Put on the full armor of God, so that you will be able to stand firm against the schemes of the devil (Ephesians 6:10).

We need ischus to confront family problems or personal conflicts. We need ischus to speak the truth in love. We need ischus to stand up to our convictions. We need ischus to go for counseling and confront our demons.

The five powers of God are given to us so that, as ambassadors, we'll represent the King well. We'll also expand His influence around the world.

God, please fill us with the 6th set of keys—power.

ENDNOTES

1. *Ginosko*, NT: Strong's #1097

2. See my book, *Jesus, I Want to Know Him*, to learn how to build an intimate relationship with Jesus.

17
MANIFESTATIONS OF THE HOLY SPIRIT

The Gifts of the Spirit

Earlier we identified talents and the gifts of the Holy Spirit as the 6th key. Although most people equate the gifts with church services, nothing could be further from the truth. They're designed to be used everywhere. The gifts of the Spirit are for the streets, the offices and your home. The gifts can be used to convince a non-believer or navigate a tough problem.

> *But if all prophesy, and an unbeliever or an uninformed person comes in, he is convinced by all, he is convicted by all. And thus the secrets of his heart are revealed; and so, falling down on his face, he will worship God and report that God is truly among you (1 Corinthians 14:24-25).*

The gifts of the Spirit are for today. After 29 years of being a leader, I've discovered that the gifts are largely ignored, abused, misused or misunderstood. Let's take a few moments to have a fresh look at them from God's Word.

> *But the manifestation of the Spirit is given to each one for the profit of all: for to one is given the word of wisdom through the Spirit, to another the word of knowledge through the same Spirit, to another faith by the same Spirit, to*

another gifts of healings by the same Spirit, to another the working of miracles, to another prophecy, to another discerning of spirits, to another different kinds of tongues, to another the interpretation of tongues. But one and the same Spirit works all these things, distributing to each one individually as He wills (1 Corinthians 12:7-11).

This scripture opened my eyes to the proper perspective and application of the gifts. Notice the word Paul used to set the whole context of the gifts: the *manifestation* of the Spirit.

The Greek word for *manifestation* is "phanerósis." It means to *make known, disclose, a coming to light.*

I believe that a *manifestation* of the Spirit is hugely different from someone's *reaction* to the Holy Spirit. People react in all kinds of interesting ways. Some fall, some cry, some roll on the ground, some fall to their knees, some have a type of open vision, and others laugh. These are all reactions. Unfortunately, I've heard many people concentrate entirely on such things while others see them as "proof" that the gifts aren't real. Both extremes are incorrect and harmful to the body of Christ.

The scripture made it clear. The Holy Spirit will manifest in the following ways:
- words of wisdom
- words of knowledge
- faith
- prophecy
- discerning of spirits
- gifts of healings
- working of miracles
- speaking in tongues
- interpretation of tongues

Do you think that these gifts might be handy to expand God's Kingdom on earth? I do.

Do you think that the gift of discernment could help you in your business, in your next home purchase, or in the signing of your next contract? I think so! How about a word of knowledge or a word of wisdom? A word of knowledge can give you inside-information on parenting, investments, real estate, the needs of others, or a host of other things. A word of wisdom can prevent severe mistakes. It can help you lay a firm foundation for a marriage or ministry.

What about the working of miracles or gifts of healing? Have your co-workers or neighbors ever needed a miracle or a healing? God is just waiting for you to step up so that He can show off. He wants to pour His favors through you. He wants you to be the light of the world and the salt of the earth.

Unfortunately, many don't even allow this type of divine expression within their congregations. But for those of us that do, we must take a step of faith to *loose* the gifts from the confinement of our churches. Friends, we have an unfair advantage over everyone in the world. Not only are we destined to go to heaven, we have the tools to bring some of heaven to this earth.

How about it? Don't you think we need more heaven on this planet? Wouldn't you like to be used by the Holy Spirit to touch lives with the gifts that He's deposited in you?

A few years ago, I met a successful businessman who was thinking of entering the political arena. We became friends. He introduced me to President Bush and several other political leaders. We spent time talking about The Lord, politics and, of course, family. One night, I had a very specific dream about him. A man was trying to become his friend and sponsor, but in the dream, this man was colluding with corrupt operations.

When I woke up that morning, I knew it was from The Lord, but I hesitated to share it with him. We didn't know each other *that* well, and he wasn't familiar with the gifts.

As I was getting a coffee at the drive-thru, I felt impressed to call him. After some small talk, I asked him if I could share my dream. I explained that sometimes I get dreams that are from God, and I felt the need to share it with him. Afterwards, he could tell me if it was indigestion (a bad taco) or God.

The Bible says, *"we know in part and we prophesy in part"* (1 Corinthians 13:9). The gifts aren't a sledge hammer; they're to be shared in humility. We could be wrong, so let's admit that from the start. Trust me, it takes all the pressure off of you.

So, I shared the dream with him and waited for a response. Silence! Then I started back pedaling, giving him room to tell me that I was wrong, but his response confirmed the dream. After a while he said, "No, no pastor, it's right on. How did you know?"

He'd been warned by one other person that the potential financial backer was connected to organized crime.

I told him that God must love him so much to give me a dream like that. Shortly after, he gave his life to Christ. I love the gifts of the Spirit.

Key #9: The Fruit of the Spirit

But the fruit of the Spirit is love, joy, peace, longsuffering, kindness, goodness, faithfulness, gentleness, and self-control. Against such there is no law (Galatians 5:22-23).

The term "fruit of the Spirit" means exactly that: it's the fruit that is produced in us when we're filled with the Spirit. If we walk in the Spirit and abide in the Spirit, we'll bear the fruit of the Spirit. We'll produce something that is attractive to a Christ-less world. The Father has always wanted us to bear much fruit:

I am the vine, you are the branches. He who abides in Me, and I in him, bears much fruit; for without Me you can do nothing. If anyone does not abide in Me, he is cast out as a branch and is withered; and they gather them and throw them into the fire, and they are burned. If you abide in Me, and My words abide in you, you will ask what you desire, and it shall be done for you. By this My Father is glorified, that you bear much fruit; so you will be My disciples (John 15:5-8).

The fruit of the Spirit is exactly what the world needs but can't find. The world keeps looking for love in all the wrong places. When we're led by the Spirit of Jesus that lives in us, we'll demonstrate these incredible qualities. People will be drawn to us like magnets. The Spirit-led life is still a battle because we still live in the flesh. It's a daily battle to take every thought captive and say no to the lust of the eyes, the lust of the flesh and the pride of life.

But a Spirit-led life will produce fruit, which is *evidence* of the Spirit. This will cause us to have favor with God and man, promotions, and influence. Favor will be our harvest.

So continuing daily with one accord in the temple, and breaking bread from house to house, they ate their food with gladness and simplicity of heart, praising God and having favor with all the people. And the Lord added to the church daily those who were being saved (Acts 2:46-47).

Jabez also prayed for this type of harvest in 1 Chronicles 4:10:

And Jabez called on the God of Israel saying, "Oh, that You would bless me indeed, and enlarge my territory, that Your hand would be with me, and that You would keep me from evil, that I may not cause pain!" So God granted him what he requested.

Jabez's platform was his honor. God could trust him with blessings and expansion because he had a firm foundation. The gifts of the Spirit can gain you success and fame, but only character can help you keep it and pass it down to the next generation. The fruit of the Spirit is a character that has been transformed by a willing person and a willing God. The world is dying to see real Christians, real power, real gifts and real character. In fact, all of creation is waiting for it.

For we know that the whole creation groans and labors with birth pangs together until now. Not only that, but we also who have the first fruits of the Spirit, even we ourselves groan within ourselves, eagerly waiting for the adoption, the redemption of our body (Romans 8:22-23).

You and I are sons and daughters of God. We've been given His Spirit and His gifts. Now it's time to seize the keys that He wants us to use for His glory and the expansion of the Kingdom of heaven.

18
THE KINGDOM OF GOD HAS COME UPON YOU

But Jesus knew their thoughts, and said to them: "Every kingdom divided against itself is brought to desolation, and every city or house divided against itself will not stand. If Satan casts out Satan, he is divided against himself. How then will his kingdom stand? And if I cast out demons by Beelzebub, by whom do your sons cast them out? Therefore they shall be your judges. But if I cast out demons by the Spirit of God, surely the Kingdom of God has come upon you" (Matthew 12:25-28).

I strategically use the gifts of the Spirit to influence the lost and win people to Christ. I use them to become like Barnabas: the son of encouragement. I've had so much fun using the fruit of the Spirit in our ministry in France. It's not about fancy programs or slick marketing. We went to France and just loved them.

The will of God is to use people like you and me to bring the Kingdom of God to this broken world. If the world experiences a little or a lot of heaven, don't you think they'll want more? Perhaps they'll even want to go there one day! Give them a foretaste of perfect peace, love, unity and power because if they taste some of what God's kingdom has to offer, I'm convinced they'll want to know the Ruler of that Kingdom. *We represent Him.* If we pour our lives out to seek first the Kingdom of God, we *will* influence the kingdoms of this world.

We need to help our children understand that a complete surrender to Christ doesn't mean they have to become missionaries or senior pastors. 100% surrender to Christ may mean that they found the next Microsoft or create a new dance style that will rock society. Perhaps they'll build a multimillion dollar company that will fund their church or inner city outreach. Perhaps, filled with the power of God, they'll be launched into professional athletics or ground-breaking humanitarian efforts. Will the next Rembrandt or Monet come out of our Sunday school classes? Will the next Mother Teresa come out of our youth groups? Will the next great doctor come out of our nurseries? What about our next president or a general for our military?

What will be the fruit of all the outpourings of the Holy Spirit? We've experienced some serious moves in the past ten years. What churches will arise to change the world like the Church of Jerusalem? What businesses will evolve? What great justice issue will be fought? I don't believe we've been clear about the character of the Holy Spirit and the "then what" once people have experienced His presence. We've confined Him to the church buildings instead of releasing our congregations into the world to change it with Holy Spirit power.

In Matthew 12, Jesus was confronted by the Pharisees,

Now when the Pharisees heard it they said, "This fellow does not cast out demons except by Beelzebub, the ruler of the demons" (Matthew 12:24).

Are we afraid of being misunderstood? or falsely accused? When we step up for the King, we will catch some heat. The enemy of humanity will try to use people like puppets. They may turn against you.

I remember when Nini from India was placed in jail after she started a clinic in a slum area. Someone falsely accused her, and the authorities threw her in jail. Then the radical extremists burned down the clinic.

On a trip to another nation, Pasqual and I arrived to some bad news. The leaders had decided to cancel the evangelistic meetings because the extremists had threatened to throw acid bombs on me and burn down the building. As we sat around the table, I could see the fear in their eyes. But to my surprise, I felt a rush of courage and strategy filling my heart and mind.

I looked at Pasqual and said, "Pasqual are you afraid to die?"

He answered me, "No Pastor, I'm not afraid to die."

I looked at him with a confidence that could only be ischus: "Well Pasqual, nor am I. Let's do it anyway."

We sat with the pastors and shared a strategy to change the name of the events to "Meetings of Blessings." We spread the word that we had come to bless everyone in the region.

I'll never forget those meetings of blessings. The presence of God was so evident. We kept everything very positive, fun and loving. I did see a few spies enter the packed hall, only to leave a few minutes later. They must have been convinced by our love–and courage.

This is what occurs when we allow His power to flow through us. We've chosen to please the King instead of the world. We've said yes to the Holy Spirit rather than try to dumb down the Gospel. Jesus never dumbed it down. People want the power of God.

Although Jesus was sensitive to seekers, He never watered down His methods or message. Although He cared about religious people, He was committed to demonstrating what heaven is really like. Jesus basically told them that when the Kingdom of God comes upon you, watch out! He's the boss!

> But if I cast out demons by the Spirit of God, surely the Kingdom of God has come upon you. Or how can one enter a strong man's house and plunder his goods, unless he first binds the strong man? And then he will plunder his house. He who is not with Me is against Me, and he who does not gather with Me scatters abroad (Matthew 12:28-30).

Wow, when the Kingdom of God comes upon us we get delivered, healed and redeemed. If you have any doubt about God's purpose for your life or His Church, read Matthew 12:28 again. Jesus has already bound the strongman, the devil. Jesus has already taken care of the ultimate fate of satan. It's up to us to use this authority with confidence and vision.

Are you for Christ or against Him? If you're for Him, commit your life to spreading His Kingdom one person, one family, one business, one city, one school, one hospital and one nation at a time. You are the one that God wants to fill and use. He won't force you. He chooses all, but He can only use the willing.

Create A Legacy

> Hear, my children, the instruction of a father and give attention to know understanding; for I give you good doctrine: Do not forsake my law. When I was my father's son, tender and the only one in the sight of my mother, he also taught me, and said to me: "Let your heart retain my words; keep my commands, and live. Get wisdom! Get understanding! Do not forget, nor turn away from the words of my mouth" (Proverbs 4:1-5).

Although David committed his life to building the nation of Israel, he didn't forget that his son, Solomon, would be a part of his legacy.

Kingdom domination takes time. Those that have gained great wealth and power in our nation have done so over time. It's easier to change a city or a nation if you're building upon the foundations laid by godly parents or grandparents. Perhaps you're the pivotal person that God will use to cause a generational shift in your family, church or city. You can become the portal of heavenly blessings for your entire family.

In Luke 11:9, we're told that Abraham entered the Promised Land and dwelt there with Isaac and Jacob. Isaac and Jacob inherited an instrumental blessing because of their father. If the sins of the father can negatively impact generations, what happens when we live, choose, plan and give with a mindset to *bless* the generations that follow us?

The Kingdom of heaven is like a relay race. The purpose is to win for God and win for others. The transition of passing the baton from generation to generation is the most difficult part. Make sure that you are in agreement with your spouse for your next generation:

Can two walk together, unless they are agreed? (Amos 3:3).

There's an interesting relationship in the Spirit when families are united. Your years together as a family should be your finest. Learn to enjoy each other. Mentor your children and build a dynasty that can have great eternal impact. Help your children to get up in the world. Give them the advantages that they need. They'll need a nudge sometimes, and all the time they'll need love.

Paul lived his life like a runner. He knew he wasn't the only one in the race. You are, too, and there are others that have been called to run with you. Do you work well with others? Are you submitted to a local church leadership? Are you in intimate fellowship with family members?

Do you not know that those who run in a race all run, but one receives the prize? Run in such a way that you may obtain it. And everyone who competes for the prize is temperate in all things. Now they do it to obtain a perishable crown, but we for an imperishable crown. Therefore I run thus: not with uncertainty. Thus I fight: not as one who beats the air. But I discipline my body and bring it into subjection, lest, when I have preached to others, I myself should become disqualified (1 Corinthians 9:24-27).

I have fought the good fight, I have finished the race, I have kept the faith (2 Timothy 4:7).

I'm sure that Paul felt he'd run the race well. His spiritual children would take his life example and message to the furthest corners of the known world. His legacy remains steady to this day! What about your legacy? Will they say of you, "She was a world changer," or "She helped change my world"? Will friends and family look back at your life and say, "Wow, in a chaotic world they became an anchor to me." If you're given a platform of success and fame, will you give credit to a great God that filled you, blessed you and used you?

When people do well, I often hear them say, "Oh no, it's not me, it's all God." I beg to differ. I believe that you played a major role in the miracle. You could have said "no" to His leading, "no" to practicing your piano, "no" to working hard at school, or "no" to all the sacrifices it took to make a difference. The truth is very clear: if you say "yes" to Him, "yes" to hard work, "yes" to sacrifice, "yes" to His gifts, "yes" to His keys and "yes" to His Kingdom, then God will one day say, *"...Well done, good and faithful servant; you have been faithful over a few things, I will make you ruler over many things. Enter into the joy of your lord" (Matthew 25:23).*

The example of Elijah and Elisha is a perfect model for us today. If you're 40 years old or older, it's time to become an Elijah. See yourself in the context of a generational move of God. It will take generations to bring the Kingdom of heaven to the kingdoms of this world. It will take spiritual armies. The Elijahs must find the Elishas and the thousands who've not bowed down to Baal.

If you're under 40, see yourself like an Elisha. Find a man or woman of God to serve. Do it with all your heart. Find a great local church and get involved. Become a team player: unselfish, committed and full of the Spirit. Double portions are reserved for those that serve with a clean heart.

19
FROM GLORY TO GLORY

Key #10: An intimate relationship with the King

Notice that we're not talking about Elvis, the king of rock-n-roll, or Michael Jackson, the king of pop. We're not talking about earthly princes, queens or kings at all. Years ago, I had the privilege of meeting with King Abdullah and some key Christian leaders. It was a big deal. Plenty of pomp and ceremony.

The King we're referring to is the King of kings. Intimacy with Him is a powerful key. Don't forget that our faith is built upon relationship—a relationship with Jesus, God the Father, and the Holy Spirit. And intimacy is the key...if you're intimate with Him, you'll become part of His strategy and implementation. He loves you.

> *But we all, with unveiled face, beholding as in a mirror the glory of the Lord, are being transformed into the same image from glory to glory, just as by the Spirit of the Lord (2 Corinthians 3:18).*

It may be difficult for us to comprehend that God gives us the keys to His Kingdom. He has big plans for us. He loves us. He has adopted, called, forgiven and empowered us. His ultimate purpose is for us to rule and reign with Him:

If we endure, we shall also reign with Him (2 Timothy 2:12a).

And [You] have made us kings and priests to our God; And we shall reign on the earth (Revelation 5:10).

Isn't that a tremendous promise?

He wants us to experience and receive glory. Doesn't the Bible tell us that Jesus Christ is our hope of glory?

To them God willed to make known what are the riches of the glory of this mystery among the Gentiles: which is Christ in you, the hope of glory (Colossians 1:27).

What are you hoping for? There's nothing wrong with hoping for a better life here on earth and in heaven.

And everyone who has left houses or brothers or sisters or father or mother or wife or children or lands, for My name's sake, shall receive a hundredfold, and inherit eternal life (Matthew 19:29).

Sacrifice will produce awesome benefits! God wants us to feel excited about our futures. The Christian walk is not about an endless stream of sufferings and sacrifices and misery. All of our sufferings and sacrifices are for one ultimate goal. That is so amazing. We get to rule and reign with Him. We get to share in His glory. We get to taste of the heavenly blessings. I've mentioned that there are over 100 billion stars and over 100 billion galaxies in the universe. When Jesus said, *I go to prepare a place for you,* could it be that He was talking about the heavens; i.e., *all* of the heavens? Scientists tell us that the universe keeps expanding by some invisible force. Could that force be Jesus Christ? Colossians 1:15-18 seems to endorse this concept:

He is the image of the invisible God, the firstborn over all creation. For by Him all things were created that are in heaven and that are on earth, visible and invisible, whether thrones or dominions or principalities or powers. All things were created through Him and for Him. And He is before all things, and in Him all things consist. And He is the head of the body, the church, who is the beginning, the firstborn from the dead, that in all things He may have the preeminence.

Who else can hold it all together and expand it at the same time? Hey friends, Jesus is so huge, He can handle all of our little challenges.

Who knows what God has in store for His elect, His chosen, His redeemed? That's us, friends! 1 Corinthians 2:9 says it so well,

But as it is written: Eye has not seen, nor ear heard, nor have entered into the heart of man the things which God has prepared for those who love Him.

Do you need more proof that God wants to bring you from glory to glory? Trials and temptations are simply delays to our ultimate destiny. Jeremiah 29:11 has always been one of my favorite verses in the Bible:

For I know the thoughts that I think toward you, says the Lord, thoughts of peace and not of evil, to give you a future and a hope.

He has plans for us. Good ones. Great ones.

The Bible says that the sins of the fathers will fall on the sons for generations (see Exodus 20:5, 34:6-7, Deuteronomy 5:9). Strongholds, limitations, addictions, pride, anger and bitterness are passed down from generation to generation. They originate from families; but also from racial, cultural, and natural sources. That's why Paul said, *"For we do not wrestle against flesh and blood, but against principalities, against powers, against the rulers of the darkness of this age, against spiritual hosts of wickedness in the heavenly places" (Ephesians 6:12).*

Satan's goal is always to steal, kill and destroy. He wants to help perpetuate the battles of our past.

Please take a look at the "Modified Model of the Mind" below. My mentor, Dr. Dobbins, taught me the Model of the Mind in 1983. I've used it personally. I've also applied it to my counseling practice and with the leadership of ICLV. I've made a few modifications to help you see that God wants you to hear His voice. But so does the father of all lies.

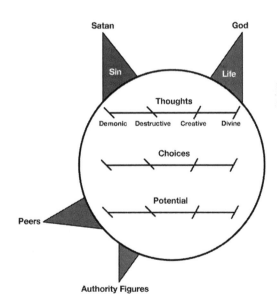

Your Vat

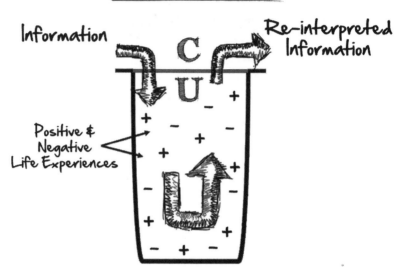

The "Modified Model of the Mind" illustrates the battle that goes on in our minds. Every day, satan speaks to your mind to influence your thoughts, choices and actions, which will lead you to your destructive or demonic potential. We all have the ability to say and do horrible things that perpetuate the curses, prejudices and mistakes from the past.

"The Vat," also pictured above, represents all of our past experiences and perceptions, which affect how we "filter" information in the present. If we've collected negativity in our vat, and if we fail to clean it out through healing and repentance, then we'll view everything in life based on these negative experiences. This causes us to misinterpret the events of our lives. We don't live with the facts of our life but the *interpretation* of the facts of our lives.

God, on the other hand, speaks to your mind to think thoughts, make choices and take actions that will lead you to your creative, divine potential. We all have seeds of greatness, kindness, love, creativity and gifts in us. We all have the potential for good—very good. This is why we must take every thought captive and have our minds transformed (see 2 Corinthians 10:5, Romans 12:2).

In order to make choices that will usher the Kingdom of heaven into our families, homes and beyond, we'll need to win the war in our minds.

This is the secret of how we can move from glory to glory to glory. There are no permanent lids in our lives, only levels. God's plan for us is glory to glory. He wants to give us the keys to accomplish this vision. It's up to us to seize these amazing gifts to fulfill His plan for our lives and nations. As you read this book, He's throwing you the keys that can transform families, cities and even continents. It's up to you.

Will you give yourself fully to:

1. seek His Kingdom?
2. bring His Kingdom to this earth?
3. activate the keys He is offering you?

Never despise small steps or small victories. Small progress is still progress. Success creates movement. Movement creates momentum. I've often told my friends and family that I've had an amazing ride since I gave myself to partner with the King of kings. I dare you to grab the keys of His Kingdom and take 'em for a ride.

I urge you in the sight of God who gives life to all things, and before Christ Jesus who witnessed the good confession before Pontius Pilate, that you keep this commandment without spot, blameless until our Lord Jesus Christ's appearing, which He will manifest in His own time, He who is the blessed and only Potentate, the King of kings and Lord of lords, who alone has immortality, dwelling in unapproachable light, whom no man has seen or can see, to whom be honor and everlasting power. Amen (1 Timothy 6:13-16).

CONCLUSION

The staff at the International Church of Las Vegas is dedicated to helping you discover the keys of the Kingdom. We invite you to join us at ICLV.com to enjoy live streaming, free archives and more. We offer tons of free programming, inspirational worship, teachings and training. On Sundays at 9:00 a.m., 11:00 a.m., and 5:00 p.m., our services are live from Las Vegas. I invite you to join the great move of God that is flowing through ICLV.

If you're interested in leadership training and certification, please check out our online Academy of Leadership.

If you feel called to full-time ministry, or you just need more training, our Kairos School of Ministry offers a 9-month, full-time schedule; a summer intensive; a fully accredited university degree; and internships. Our vision is to plant 2,000 churches by the year 2020. We're looking for students of all ages who want to make a difference in the world. Our graduating students may also apply for mission opportunities in India, Mexico, Africa, Canada, and Europe. The fields are indeed *white unto harvest*. All of our students are trained in Bible study, the prophetic, miracles, the Holy Spirit, preaching, leadership, worship and pastoral ministry in general.

Internship opportunities are available for qualified students who are looking for further hands-on training.

Our city vision includes the Summerlin campus that houses our preschool, grades K-8, Kairos School of Ministry and many other church ministries. Our Dream Center meets the needs of the Las Vegas inner city. It's a wonderful place where teams from all across America come to help in the heart of Las Vegas. Our South Gate campus is an exciting place where miracles and outreaches happen weekly. Our newest campus is Prayer Mountain. It's reaching a whole new segment of Las Vegas with a huge counseling center. The power of prayer is on all campuses. As you already know, prayer is another key that we didn't talk a lot about in the book. There are so many amazing books on this subject that I'll let people like Reese Howells take us to school. His book, *Intercessor*, is one of my favorites.

If you would like to know more about the many resources in our bookstore or the ministries of our church, please visit our website and interact with our staff at ICLV.com.

If you're interested in being credentialed as a minister, or if you're looking for a ministry covering, please contact the International Network of Commissioned Workers at incwonline.com

May God richly bless you in the years to come and may you seize the keys of the Kingdom for God's glory.

ABOUT PAUL GOULET

Paul Goulet is the senior pastor of ICLV, a multicultural church with campuses throughout the Las Vegas valley and online that reach thousands each week. He and his wife, Denise, have 3 children, 5 grandchildren, and 2 sons from Africa - all working together for the advancement of the Kingdom. For more information on Pastor Paul, visit ICLV.com and connect with us on Twitter @ICLV.

ADDITIONAL TITLES BY PAUL GOULET

Vision Bible
Crossing Your Next Threshold
5 Powers of God
The Transformed Family
The Power of Impartation
Jesus, I Want to Know You
30 Day Journey Series

45511095R00074

Made in the USA
Charleston, SC
22 August 2015